COCONUT
&
SAMBAL

LARA LEE

COCONUT & SAMBAL

RECIPES FROM MY INDONESIAN KITCHEN

BLOOMSBURY

LONDON · OXFORD · NEW YORK · NEW DELHI · SYDNEY

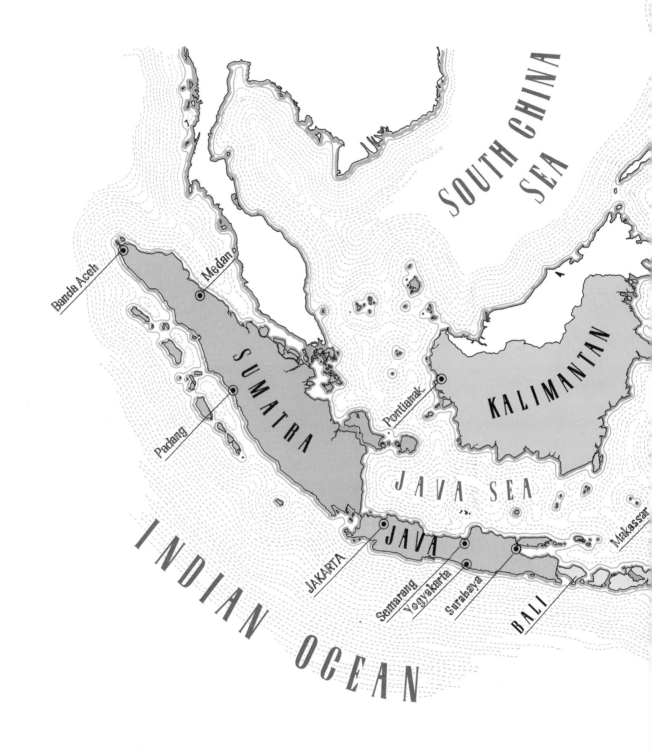

SOUTH CHINA SEA

Banda Aceh

Medan

SUMATRA

Padang

Pontianak

KALIMANTAN

JAVA SEA

Makassar

JAKARTA

JAVA

Semarang

Yogyakarta

Surabaya

BALI

INDIAN OCEAN

| 0 | 250 | 500 | 750 km |

| 0 | 250 | 500 mi |

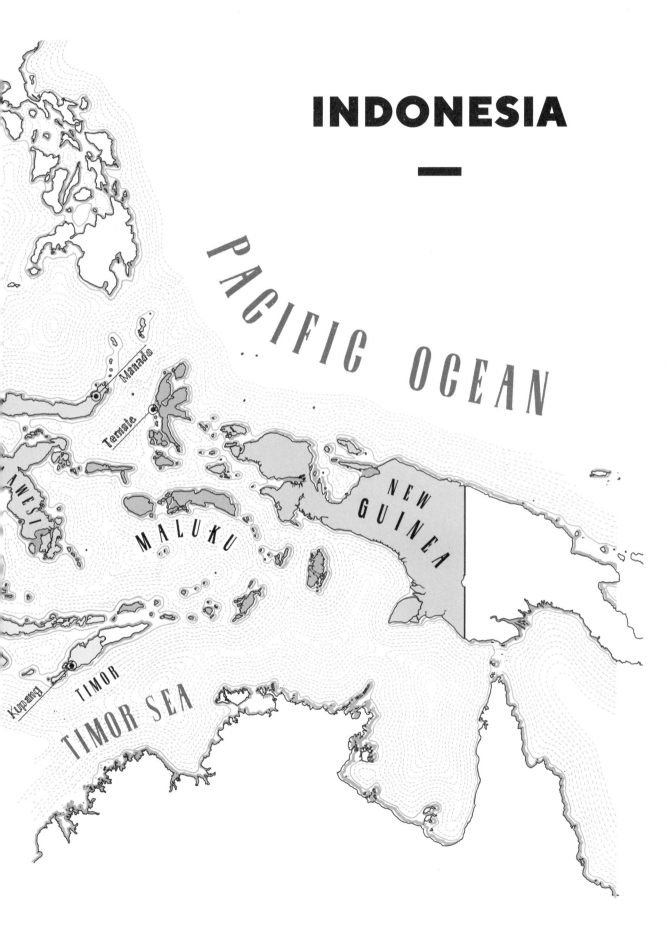

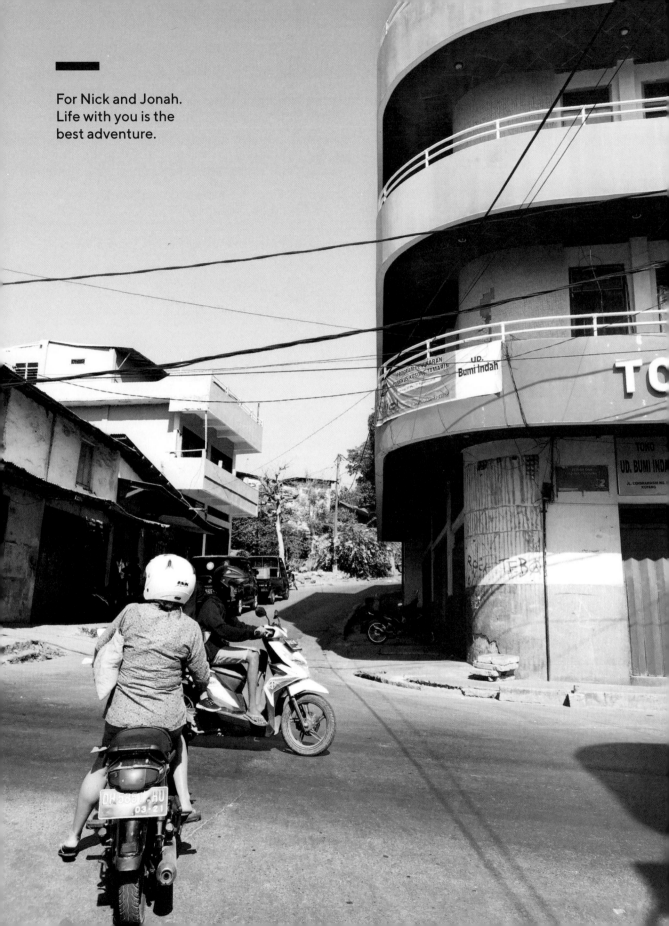

For Nick and Jonah.
Life with you is the
best adventure.

ACROSS THE TIMOR SEA

The first time I watched the sky bleed tones of orange and red as the sun set over the sea in my father's home town of Kupang, Timor, it struck me as a moment of coming home – but to a place I had never been before. A bustling collective of food vendors dotted the shoreline, the smoke from their coal and wood fires blurring the glowing horizon, the fragrance of lemongrass, kaffir lime and garlic filling the air. The pier, where local fishermen waited for their catch of the day to bite, was stained with splashes of black, the last ink squirts of life from squid and cuttlefish attempting to escape their captors. Surrounding the pier were the winding narrow streets that made up the old town, home to an eclectic mix of worn, tiled and rainbow-coloured terraces. There, where shops lined the ground floor with the owners' homes perched above, was my grandmother's house, the place where my story begins.

My earliest memories of Indonesia occurred outside of it, across the Timor Sea and over land in Sydney, Australia. My family and I started visiting Indonesia only when I reached adulthood; before that, my grandmother Margaret Thali, who we called Popo, brought her Indonesian home to Sydney when she came to live with us. When we were young girls, my mother would dress my sister and me in batik on special occasions: vibrant, wax-patterned dyed fabric that showcased the intricate handiwork of Indonesian artisans. It was a gift to us from Popo, who wanted to clothe us in our heritage. Indonesian folk music would play on the record player, breathing melodies called *keroncong*. Our living room was filled with honeyed vocals, ukuleles, flutes and guitars; songs of lost loves and Indonesian island life that put sand between your toes.

My childhood mealtimes were filled with sausage rolls and peanut sauce – not a classic Indonesian combination, but one that sums up the influence of growing up with an Australian mother and a Chinese-Indonesian father. Popo's recipes wove themselves seamlessly into our repertoire of recipes and onto our dining table. The usual Australian fare of sausages, steaks and salads cooked on the barbecue by my parents was joined by unmissable chicken satay basted in kecap manis (sweet soy sauce) and lime. I remember watching Popo grinding the ingredients for her creamy peanut sauce to a paste before she generously drizzled it over vegetables and boiled eggs for her *gado-gado* salad (p.92). I was mesmerised by the steam that rose from her pot of *babi kecap* (p.175): cubed pork belly bubbling in a rich bath of garlic, shallots, chilli and kecap manis. Back then I was too young to learn her recipes, but the flavours of Popo's food

My grandparents, Margaret (Popo) and Liong

My parents, Jono and Coralie

My husband, Nick, and me

My sister, Katrina, and me, dressed in batik

Margaret and Liong as a young couple

left an impression that stayed with me long after she moved back to Timor and later passed away.

Many years later, when I first stepped inside Popo's vacated home in Kupang, I felt an unanticipated sense of our kinship. Our parallel lives, set decades apart, unveiled themselves first through our shared love of colour as I walked the brightly painted hallways of the family home where my father and his three sisters spent their early years. Her kitchen was every shade of blue imaginable; an azure stair handrail matched the colour of the tiles, the walls were painted a deeper cobalt blue, a blue hosepipe coiled around a blue hook on the wall. Old buckets and utensils left scattered across the room boasted further shades of blue. On the ground floor was a hallway entirely coloured pink, the floor above it purple, her bedroom lime green. It was then clear that our shared passion for food was matched by our fondness for colour.

Old black-and-white photos decorated the walls, some of my grandfather, a mirror image of my father. A framed portrait of Popo as a young woman sat atop one of the crumbling walls, the light from the window illuminating her face. Nicknamed the 'rose of Kupang', Popo was a great beauty who had many suitors for her hand, but it was my grandfather, Ang Tju Liong, who eventually won her heart. Tall, handsome, well educated and with a strong backhand in tennis, he was also the first man in Kupang to own a motorbike, no less than a Ducati. Popo and Liong met and fell in love around the time the Japanese invaded Timor during World War II, and after a short courtship they married.

When Popo was just 36 years old, my grandfather passed away suddenly from a heart attack. A young widow with four children to support, she taught herself to cook using recipe books her brother had brought from East Java to occupy her in her mourning. Popo began first to sell bread and then later cakes, known as *kue* in Indonesian, transforming her talent for cooking into a livelihood by opening a bakery on the ground floor of the four-storey family terrace. To this day, so many relics of her life remain in that home: her bed and dressing table, a chest of old photo albums, a collection of ornaments – ranging from porcelain cats to Jesus plates – and shelves of near-forgotten books. From these shelves, Popo's old recipe books, yellowed with age and stained with splashes of oil from years of use, were saved by my aunties. Indonesians typically pass their recipes down orally, from generation to generation, and while Popo taught her recipes to my aunties in this way, she also kept a written record of the recipes she used in the bakery.

It was not until I took up cooking as a profession that my desire to trace my family's culinary heritage became a mission. I longed for the funny coloured cakes Popo had made for me in my childhood, and the sweet and spicy sauces that stuck to my little hands at the end of family meals. I embarked on a journey that took me from the west coast of Sumatra to Timor in the east, where our

Popo at her bakery, Toko Surabaya, in Kupang

Popo's kitchen in Kupang, Timor

Popo and her children (from left to right): Linda, Lily, my father Jono and Kristina

family's story began. I heard the tales of our family history told by my aunties, cousins and great aunties alike. Through the pages of her recipe books, the flavours of Popo's life were recreated by my aunties' hands as we measured, rolled, mixed and created meals together. It was Popo's food that united us, and over food that we laughed and remembered. This joy compelled me to extend the search beyond my own family and to learn the recipes of the many other wonderful people I encountered as I travelled across the Indonesian archipelago in pursuit of culinary stories, of recipes passed down through generations. I was invited into strangers' kitchens, where I was treated as a family member, and left hours later having been gifted recipes that had never before been shared with outsiders. This book catalogues the recipes I learnt in the far-flung places I visited and all those family culinary treasures born in Popo's house long ago in Kupang, across the Timor Sea.

THE HEART OF INDONESIAN COOKING

Sit at any Indonesian table and you will find both coconut and sambal, a chilli sauce used to season food in the same way we might use salt and pepper in Western cuisine. While growing up in Timor, my father could not remember a meal that didn't feature sambal and his chilli tolerance is extremely high as a result, a trait I have inherited. At the heart of sambal are the fiery flames of chilli peppers, seasoned with a mix of ingredients that includes tomatoes, shallots, garlic, ginger, tamarind and *terasi* (fermented shrimp paste), among many others. The basic principle of a sambal is to provide a good level of heat, so you will find that Indonesians rarely deseed chillies, as the seed and pith are the hottest part. However, sambal exists to complement rather than overpower the flavours in the dishes it is served with, so is eaten only a little at a time, often with every bite of food. Sambal is used not only as a condiment, but also as a spice paste, a marinade and a dipping sauce (pp.190–209).

Every home cook has their own family sambal recipe, and there are hundreds of variations across the regions, all with their own distinctive flavours and ingredients. For an Indonesian, no meal is complete without sambal, so I have offered sambal pairing suggestions for many of the dishes in this book. I've kept these pairings optional – there isn't always time to make a secondary dish when cooking – but if you have a spare fifteen minutes to whip one up, it will transport your taste buds to the heart of Indonesia.

The importance of the coconut to Indonesian domesticity became most apparent to me at the home of Pak Budi in Padang, Sumatra, a Minangkabau man whose family had offered to teach me the highlights of Minangkabau cuisine. The hissing fire in their family kitchen crackled as Pak Budi's mother, Grandma Erneti, threw the husks of coconuts over the glowing charcoal, adding an earthy smoke to the flavour of the grill. The mother of the family, Ibu Iwit, scrubbed a stain on the concrete floor with the pulp of grated coconut left over from making fresh coconut milk. Her children sipped coconut water while Grandma Erneti stir-fried a spice paste for a coconut-milk-based curry in coconut oil, seasoning it with coconut sugar made from the nectar of coconut flowers. Such a scene is not uncommon in the typical Indonesian household, where no element of the coconut is wasted. Even the shells are transformed into hardy utensils and bowls. You will find coconut in most of the recipes in this book in some capacity, whether in the form of coconut milk, coconut oil for cooking or the addition of desiccated coconut for texture.

The abundance of rice

Rice is so embedded in the food culture of Indonesians that there is a saying that if you have not eaten rice, you have not eaten. It is a symbolic food used to mark momentous occasions including births, deaths and the beginning and end of religious holidays. At mealtimes, Indonesians like to fill at least half their plate with rice, believing this amount to be part of a balanced diet. This custom was instilled thirty years ago by a government-led television campaign; since Indonesia is the world's third highest producer of rice, the government sought to encourage the nation to eat the available resources.

Never a boring affair, the preparation of rice is fascinatingly diverse. I have eaten it wrapped in banana leaf and grilled over a charcoal fire, stir-fried in *nasi goreng* (p.77), pressed into sweet sticky snacks called *klepon* using milled rice flour (p.224), and simmered in broth and reduced to a bowl of savoury porridge (p.71). In times of celebration, yellow rice is shaped into a towering cone, steamed with turmeric and aromatics to form *nasi kuning* (p.247), its golden colour symbolising wealth, health and happiness. In remote communities I was offered *arak beras*, fermented rice made into rice wine, a strong liquor that burns your throat and brings your body to full attention.

Indonesian folklore dictates that farmers must make offerings of rice at harvest time to Dewi Sri, the Indonesian goddess of rice and fertility, who represents wealth and prosperity. A group of mothers I met in Jakarta told me that the respect of Dewi Sri extends to children's mealtimes, with many parents telling their children that Dewi Sri will be angry at them if they do not finish eating all the rice on their plate. Every year during the Hindu Yadnya Kasada festival, the Tenggerese people of East Java journey to the volcanic mountain of Mount Bromo for a ceremonial tradition that includes throwing sacrifices such as rice or even livestock into the crater of the volcano to appease the deities. In Bali, beautiful woven baskets called *banten saiban* can be found on every street corner. The folded rectangular banana leaves are filled with rice, flowers, food and even cigarettes, and are offered daily to thank the gods and ancestors for their blessings. Rice is life to Indonesians, providing jobs, food and protection.

Stimulating the senses

The unmistakable crunch of crackers heralds the commencement of a meal in Indonesia. These are *kerupuk*, savoury fried crackers not dissimilar to the prawn crackers found in Chinese restaurants, which stimulate the appetite. Few meals in Indonesia are served without them. In restaurants, the chaotic rhythm of cracking, crunching and snapping fills the room as diners revel in the sounds of the nationally beloved snack. Hundreds of variations are found all over the islands, from coiled rings as large as your hand to puffed beef tendons, brittle crimped squares and others that resemble potato crisps. *Kerupuk* are made with a host of umami flavours like squid, prawn, garlic and indigenous nuts, and each has its own distinctive crunch and texture when snapped, eaten and shared. Shops specialising in *kerupuk* appear in every market place, with vertical technicolour walls of cracker-filled bags as large as pillow cases hung and stacked against each other.

Visit any home cook's kitchen and you will soon become familiar with the Indonesian word *wangi*, which means 'aroma'. There is a clear purpose to every core ingredient found in Indonesian spice pastes, and when they are ground and pan-fried, their fragrance awakens the senses: the stinging burn in the air from the heat of the chilli, the citrus of lemongrass, the peppery sharpness of ginger and the savoury warmth of garlic, each one releasing essences that fill a room with *wangi*. When I was travelling, there was a moment in every cooking session when the home cook and I would bow our heads to the wok and cup the air and smoke from the pan into our lungs. When the fragrance of the spices hit, we would smile and nod at each other, knowing that we were well on our way to a delicious meal. As the moisture in the spice paste evaporates, the hot oil in the pan begins to split from the spices, a classic Indonesian technique that tells you when the spice paste has finished cooking. It is at this highest point of fragrance that the spice paste is ready for the next stage of cooking, which may be the addition of coconut milk or other ingredients to the pan.

The spirit of community

Ingrained within Indonesian culture is generosity in sharing food, resources and time. I discovered this act of hospitality had a formal name when I met a group of home cooks with a passion for East Javanese cuisine in a kitchen in Surabaya. We spent a full day cooking local recipes such as *soto ayam jawa*, tender strips of chicken bathed in a rich chicken bone broth flavoured with Indonesian spices and served with boiled eggs, vermicelli noodles, greens and bean sprouts (p.68). When the day was through, they refused any reimbursement for their time or ingredients and instead presented me with gifts typical of East Java: locally made palm sugar and a large wooden platter carved from a 100-year-old teak tree. For this group of friends, volunteering their time and gifting me with treasures of the region was an expression of friendship and long-established custom. One of the home cooks, Ibu Ley Hoen, told me: 'It is *gotong royong*.' Her friend Ratna elaborated: 'It's village philosophy – the idea of working together, of helping our friends and neighbours when they need us. We apply it to our everyday lives.'

The concept of *gotong royong*, a sense of collective responsibility within a community, originated in agriculture, where neighbouring farmers all worked together to irrigate or harvest a rice field, and is now widespread all over

Indonesia, extending well beyond farming communities. The phrase *gotong royong* hails from Java but bears a different name in other regions, such as *subak* in Bali or *mapulus* in Sulawesi.

Anyone who has visited Indonesia will have encountered the generous hospitality of its people. My experience of this extended far beyond the reaches of those tropical isles on one autumnal day in Wimbledon, south London, at the home of Sri Owen. Known as the doyenne of Indonesian cuisine, Sri is a West-Sumatran-born food writer who introduced the world to the food of her island home with the publication in 1976 of the first English-language Indonesian cookbook. I had introduced myself via email, desperately wanting to learn more about Indonesian food. With my family far away on the other side of the world, I lacked a mentor to guide my way. Sri replied immediately, inviting me to her home that weekend. When I arrived, a petite figure, standing no taller than five feet high and now in her eighties, answered the door. 'Now go wash your hands, dear,' Sri said as she popped an apron over my head, announcing that we were cooking an Indonesian feast for twelve guests who were to arrive in three hours. From that day forward, we met every week for nearly a year, cooking and testing Indonesian dishes for a variety of guests and friends who would join us for lunch with her husband, Roger. Sri's generosity and willingness to connect me to my culinary heritage primed me for the next stage of my journey: recipe research on Indonesian soil.

The emerald of the equator

Home to orangutans and komodo dragons, and one of the world's most bio-diverse nations, Indonesia lies on both sides of the equator, and is a country of dry seasons and life-giving monsoon rains. Boasting more volcanoes than any other country, its terrain ranges from snow-capped mountains to rainforests, beaches, swamps and irrigated rice fields. Dutch author Eduard Douwes Dekker wrote that Indonesia was as green as an emerald thanks to its lush natural landscape.

A scattering of more than 17,000 islands attracted traders from all over the world, bringing intellectual and cultural exchange between the 600 spoken languages and 300 ethnic groups that reside there. With the travellers came the rise and fall of Hindu, Christian, Buddhist and Islamic kingdoms, and a constant movement of people along the maritime spice route that follows the coastlines to the Maluku islands in the north-east, the birthplace of high-value native spices of mace, nutmeg, cloves and pepper, which grow in abundance. A young nation, Indonesia only declared itself a republic in 1945 following the end of World War II, giving it independence from the Dutch, although parts of Indonesia have been subject to the rule of Portugal, Britain and Japan throughout history.

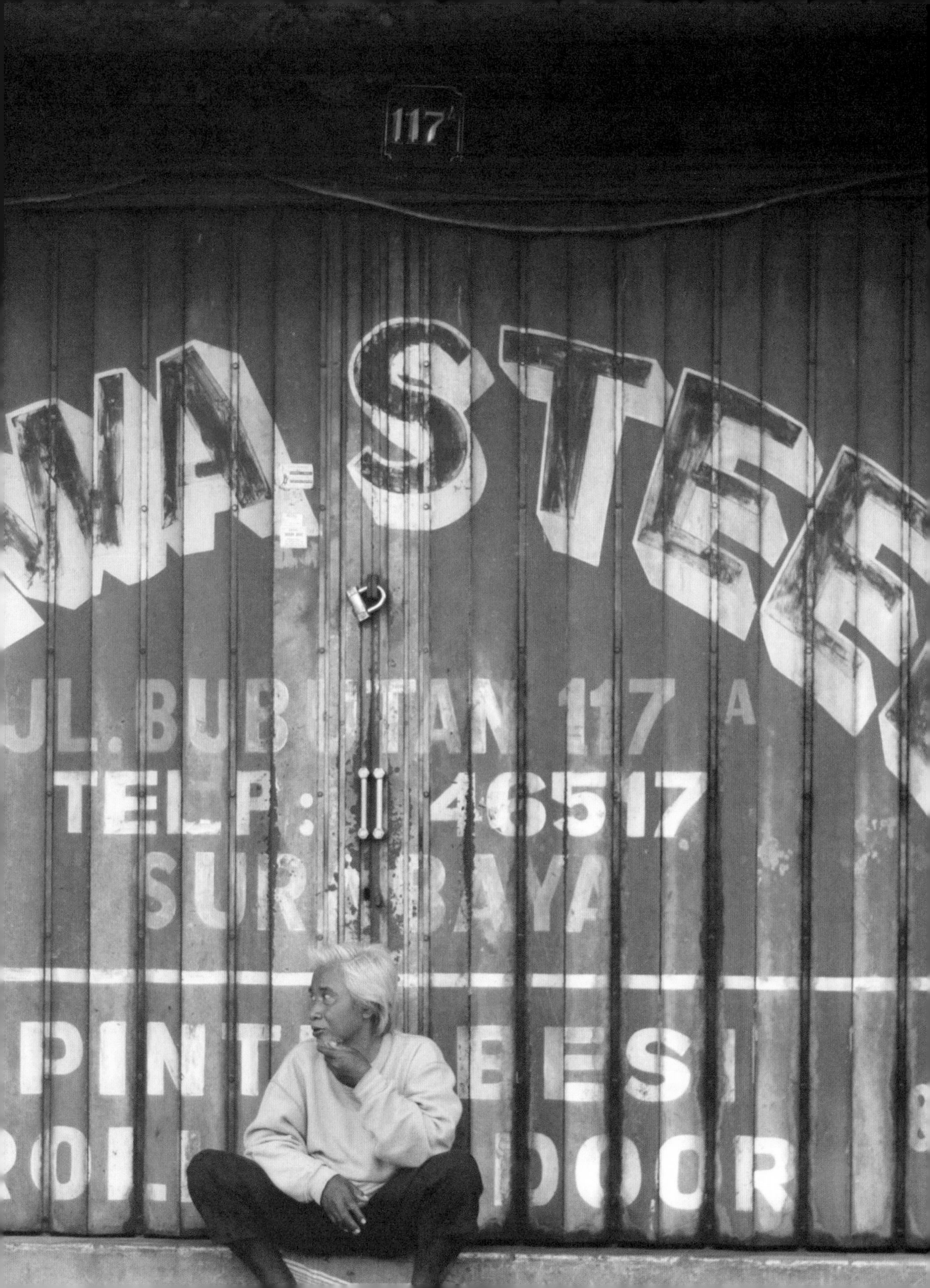
117
TELP: 46517

Despite its geographical spread, shifting colonial rule and linguistic, cultural, religious and ethnic differences, the country is far from fragmented. Its differences are embraced in the national motto, *bhinneka tunggal ika*, a Javanese expression meaning 'out of many, one', or unity in diversity. You'll find Indonesians most strongly identify with the region they are from, such as the Minahasan people of North Sulawesi or the Batak people of North Sumatra, and yet on Independence Day on 17 August every year, Indonesians everywhere proudly show their patriotism. Buildings and streets are adorned with red and white streamers and festoons of paper flowers mirroring the colours of the national flag.

A gateway to my heritage

Writing this book has been a journey of self-discovery that has helped me to understand the part of myself I never knew, immersing myself in and embracing Indonesian culture in a way that has since become a vital part of my identity. The dishes you will discover in the following pages form a connection to my heritage that has given my cooking meaning. I hope the aromas and tastes of these recipes will delight you as much as they have me, from the spice pastes that transform roast chicken or pork into an exotic and luscious feast, to the addition of coconut to simple vegetable side dishes to add texture, richness and body, or the addictive burn of sambal that brings life to any meal. The time I spent in kitchens with my Indonesian family and with the generous strangers I met during my travels has turned into an impassioned mission to share Indonesian cuisine, in all its splendour, with the rest of the world. I hope this book will inspire your home cooking, and that coconut and sambal will never be far away from your kitchen table.

SAVOURY SNACKS

—

It's fascinating to watch the street-food vendors of Indonesia. The chefs in the outdoor markets work at intense speeds, grilling, fanning and frying their offerings, always surrounded by a busy queue of happily chatting diners. The sounds of eating – from the snap of peanut and kaffir lime leaf *rempeyek* crackers (p.28) to the crisp crunch of pork and prawn pan-fried *chai kue* dumplings (p.43), which are drizzled in fragrant garlic oil and crunchy fried garlic shavings – fill the market with an electric atmosphere. Young families and friends gather for a delicious and inexpensive night out, enjoying the vast array of savoury snacks on offer.

You'll find *martabak* (pp.36–40), a blistered, pan-fried flatbread encasing local ingredients and flavours, in every city in Indonesia, where chefs create a show for the locals who swarm to stalls for their snack fix. The soft, stretchy dough of *martabak* is massaged on a table with oil before being flung and pulled into a translucent sheet as large as a family-sized pizza, which is then filled, folded and fried in a cast-iron pan. Fillings vary, but most vendors sell versions containing egg and spring onion or spiced chicken, lamb or beef.

I always remember watching my grandmother's hands as she made Indonesian *kroket* (p.50), a derivative of the Dutch croquette from colonial times. Her precision and speed in covering the spiced mince with the flattened, seasoned mix of mashed potato was hypnotic to watch. Her hands swiftly moved the *kroket* from the flour to the eggs and then the breadcrumbs in a rhythmic beat, before it was fried and given to me as a snack as soon as it was cool enough to eat.

Savoury snacks in Indonesia are more than just an appetiser before dinner; they are eaten throughout the day and form part of the social fabric that weaves Indonesian relationships together. Snacking helps to create an atmosphere of *nongkrong*, which essentially means to hang out and talk with friends over hot drinks and snacks, such as boxes of freshly fried spring rolls filled with minced, garlicky chicken (p.46) or moreish kaffir-lime-fragrant rounds of crunchy corn fritters (p.32). It is a forum for the exchange of knowledge and an outlet that helps people laugh, relax and form close bonds. At my aunty Linda's home, freshly baked buttery cheese biscuits called *kue keju* (p.30), made to my grandmother's recipe, sit at the centre of the table whenever we sip coffee together and chat as a family. It's a tradition that my aunties still follow to this day: a box of the biscuits is often presented when they host or visit.

Following Indonesia's love of *gorengan* (fried things) and stemming from a long history of frying as a cooking technique, many recipes in this chapter are fried. In outdoor kitchens where only a wok and fire are available, oil is an inexpensive cooking ingredient that helps produce crispy textures that stimulate the appetite, and frying is a way of refreshing food that might deteriorate in the powerful heat where no refrigeration is available. For those who aren't comfortable with deep-frying in their kitchens at home, I've included alternative methods of shallow pan-frying and baking where possible. These recipes are fantastic appetisers to start a dinner party or as snacks to share with friends, and some, such as the egg and spring onion *martabak* (p.36), stand alone as a delicious meal in themselves.

27 Savoury Snacks

PEANUT AND KAFFIR LIME KERUPUK
REMPEYEK

Rempeyek are a type of *kerupuk*: crunchy crackers eaten at Indonesian mealtimes to stimulate the appetite. This popular *kerupuk* was one of the first recipes I learnt to make at the home of the wonderful Indonesian food writer Sri Owen, who became my cookery mentor. Since our cooking sessions I have adapted our recipe and the result is these thin, slightly curled and moreish crackers that taste as delicious as they look. The addition of fragrant kaffir lime, ground coriander and the crunch of peanuts makes them utterly irresistible. Follow my method for perfectly crispy *rempeyek*, but if you prefer yours extra golden, like Sri, fry them twice for an even crunchier snack. They will keep for up to 2 weeks in an airtight container.

Origin Java
Makes 32–35

125g rice flour
75g unsalted peanuts, roughly chopped
5 kaffir lime leaves, stems removed, very
    thinly sliced
Sunflower oil, for frying

For the spice paste
2 garlic cloves, peeled and sliced
2 candlenuts or macadamia nuts (or 4 cashews
    or almonds), toasted for best flavour
2 tsp ground coriander
3cm piece of ginger (about 15g), peeled and
    finely chopped
1 tsp sea salt
Large pinch of white pepper

Place the spice paste ingredients in a pestle and mortar and grind to a fine paste (alternatively, you could use a small food processor, adding a small splash of water taken from the 225ml added below, to help grind the paste).

Place the rice flour in a mixing bowl and add the spice paste. Gradually add 225ml water, whisking vigorously after each addition to remove any lumps. The batter should have a smooth, creamy consistency. Cover the bowl and allow the batter to rest for 15 minutes in the fridge.

Once the batter has rested, fold through the peanuts and kaffir lime leaves.

Add enough oil to cover the base of a large deep pan, to the depth of about 1cm. Heat the oil to 175°C. (If you do not have a kitchen thermometer, check the oil is at temperature by adding a cube of bread; it should turn golden in 20 seconds.) Stir the batter well, then take a dessertspoonful of the batter, ensuring there are a couple of peanuts and kaffir lime leaf pieces on the spoon. Pour the batter into the hot oil to make a thin cracker, roughly 5cm in diameter. Repeat until you have as many crackers as will fit in the pan, but keeping them apart so they do not stick together.

Fry the crackers until hard at the edges, which will take a few minutes, then turn them over to brown the other side. Small holes should form inside the cracker. Once a light golden colour all over, remove from the oil with a slotted spoon and drain on a layer of paper towels. Give the batter a stir before cooking the next batch, as the rice flour can sink to the bottom of the mixture.

Store in an airtight container, separating the layers with baking parchment, to keep them crisp.

CHEESE BISCUITS
KUE KEJU

Kue keju were the first biscuits my grandmother Popo sold in her bakery, Toko Surabaya. Today, they remain a favourite in my family, a nostalgic snack still baked by my aunties. These savoury biscuits are a fantastic snack with a cup of tea or coffee, and always remind me of family coming together. The buttery, crumbly cheesiness is reminiscent of a cheese twist, Indonesian style. They will keep for up to 2 weeks in an airtight container in the fridge.

———

Origin Kupang, Timor
Makes 32–40

———

200g unsalted butter, softened
1 egg and 2 egg yolks, beaten together
1 tbsp white or dark rum (optional)
200g plain flour, sifted, plus extra to dust
1½ tbsp tapioca flour or cornflour
½ tsp sea salt
200g cheddar cheese, finely grated, plus a little
  extra for sprinkling

To glaze
2 egg yolks, lightly beaten

Beat the butter with an electric whisk until it turns pale. Add the beaten egg and egg yolks, one spoonful at a time, and continue mixing until pale and fluffy. Add the rum and beat together once more.

Add the remaining ingredients and mix together by hand very gently to pull it into a dough, but be careful not to overwork the mixture or it will become greasy. At this stage the dough should feel quite sticky.

Dust the work surface and lightly coat your hands with flour. Divide the dough into four equal pieces and roll each into a 2cm wide log. Cut each log on the diagonal into slices approximately 3cm thick. Continue to flour your hands and work surface as you shape each log. Place the biscuits on baking trays lined with baking parchment and chill in the fridge for at least 30 minutes before baking. Preheat the oven to 200°C/180°C fan/gas 6.

Once chilled, glaze the top of each biscuit with the egg yolk and sprinkle a little extra grated cheese on top. Bake on the middle shelf of the oven for 15–20 minutes or until golden. Remove from the oven and allow to cool on the tray for 5 minutes before transferring to a wire rack to cool completely.

POTATO FRITTERS
PERKEDEL KENTANG

Golden pillows fragrant with nutmeg and white pepper, these deep-fried potato fritters are crispy on the outside and fluffy within. You can pair them with most sambals, but my favourite way to eat them is with a punchy *rica-rica* chilli sauce.

The traditional cooking method, which hails from Yogyakarta, central Java, spoons the mixture into hot oil to form rustic parcels. If you're after a neater finish, however, you can roll the potato mixture into a log, wrap it tightly in cling film and freeze it, then unwrap and slice it into discs, ready to be fried. The fritters keep for up to 2 days in the fridge and, if prepared in advance, are best reheated in the oven for 10 minutes at 170°C/150°C fan/gas 3.

Origin Yogyakarta, Java
Chilli heat Mild
Makes 12–16

400g floury potatoes (such as Maris Piper), peeled and cut into chunks
1 tsp ground nutmeg
¼ tsp ground white pepper
1 tsp sea salt
1 tbsp unsalted butter, softened
3 tbsp Fried shallots (p.251)
2 eggs, beaten
Sunflower oil, for deep-frying
1 quantity of Sulawesi rica-rica chilli sauce (p.209), or sriracha chilli sauce, to serve (optional)

Place the potatoes in a large saucepan filled with salted cold water. Bring to the boil, lower the heat to a medium simmer and cook the potatoes for 15–20 minutes or until easily pierced with the tip of a knife. Drain the potatoes and return them to the hot pan for a minute or so to dry out.

Mash the potatoes in the pan until smooth and then transfer the mash to a large bowl. Add the nutmeg, pepper, salt, butter, fried shallots and beaten eggs and stir well to combine.

Fill a deep saucepan one-third full with oil. Heat the oil to 160°C. (If you do not have a kitchen thermometer, check the oil is at temperature by adding a cube of bread; it should turn golden in 25–30 seconds.) Carefully drop a dessertspoonful of the potato mixture into the hot oil. Repeat to make 6–8 fritters, without overcrowding the pan. Fry until golden all over, moving the fritters around so they don't burn. Transfer to a tray lined with paper towels to absorb any excess oil. Repeat until all the potato mixture is used, topping up the oil if necessary. Serve immediately with sambal or chilli sauce, if using.

Variation: Pan-fried potato fritters

Preheat the oven to 200°C/180°C fan/gas 6. Heat 4 tablespoons of oil in a large frying pan over a high heat. When the oil is shimmering, gently slide dessertspoonfuls of the mash into the oil and flatten each one into a disc, taking care not to overcrowd the pan. After 2–3 minutes, using a fish slice or spatula, turn the fritters over and cook until golden all over. Transfer to a baking parchment-lined baking tray and transfer to the oven for 5–10 minutes. Test one fritter to ensure it is heated through. Drain on paper towels to absorb any excess oil. Serve immediately.

SPICED CORN FRITTERS
PERKEDEL JAGUNG

My aunty Tje Ie in Kupang, Timor, loves to make these when she has visitors – a tradition I've carried over to my home in London. Juicy, chunky kernels of corn come together with fragrant spices and aromatics to form these delicious fritters. They keep for up to 2 days in the fridge and, if prepared in advance, are best reheated in the oven for 10 minutes at 170°C/150°C fan/gas 3.

If using canned or frozen corn, squeeze out as much moisture as possible – the easiest way is in between layers of paper towels.

Origin Popular all over Indonesia
Chilli heat Mild
Makes 15 large fritters

---

4 corn-on-the-cob or 350g canned or frozen
    sweetcorn kernels
1 tbsp sunflower oil, plus extra for deep-frying
6cm piece of ginger (about 30g), peeled and
    thinly sliced
6 garlic cloves, peeled and thinly sliced
2 long red chillies, thinly sliced
2 small banana shallots or 4 Thai shallots, peeled
    and thinly sliced
2 large spring onions, thinly sliced
5 kaffir lime leaves (optional), stems removed,
    very thinly sliced
2 tsp ground coriander
1 tsp ground cumin
3 pinches of sea salt
Large pinch of black pepper
2 eggs, beaten
6 tbsp cornflour
1 quantity of Tomato sambal (p.194), Fresh
    tomato and basil dabu-dabu (p.196) or sriracha
    chilli sauce, to serve (optional)

If using fresh corn, remove the outer husk and threads, then carefully slice down the outside of the cob with a knife, as close to the core as possible, to remove the kernels. Set them aside.

Heat the oil in a frying pan over a medium heat. Add the ginger, garlic, chillies and shallots and fry, stirring, for 10 minutes. Blend to a medium-fine paste in a small food processor with the spring onions and kaffir lime leaves, if using. Mix the spice paste with the corn kernels in a bowl and add the coriander, cumin, salt, pepper and eggs. Stir well to combine, then add the cornflour.

Fill a deep saucepan one-third full with oil. Heat the oil to 180°C. (If you do not have a kitchen thermometer, check the oil is at temperature by adding a cube of bread; it should turn golden in 15 seconds.) Carefully drop a dessertspoonful of the batter into the hot oil – it should settle into a roughly circular shape. Repeat to make 6–8 fritters, without overcrowding the pan. Fry until golden all over, about 4 minutes. Test one to ensure it is cooked through. Transfer to a tray lined with paper towels to drain. Repeat to use up all the mixture, topping up the oil if needed. Serve immediately, with sambal or chilli sauce to dip, if using.

Variation: Pan-fried corn fritters

Preheat the oven to 200°C/180°C fan/gas 6. Heat 4 tablespoons of oil in a large frying pan over a high heat until the oil shimmers. Add spoonfuls of the corn mixture to the oil, flattening them lightly. Turn over after 2–3 minutes – they should be golden all over. Transfer to a baking tray lined with baking parchment and cook in the oven for 5–10 minutes – test one to ensure it is cooked through. Drain any excess oil on paper towels and serve.

GRILLED SWEET CHILLI CORN
JAGUNG BAKAR

Blackened grilled corn basted with a sweet and salty chilli butter is an irresistible combination. I first tried it after leaving a beach party in the early hours of the morning in Canggu, Bali. Street-food vendors fill the lane leading to the beach, ready for all those in search of the equivalent of a kebab after a night of dancing. This corn-on-the-cob certainly hit the spot.

It takes only minutes to whip up, but it's truly satisfying. It's best eaten straight off the grill, served as a snack on its own, or as a side with a stir-fry, roast or fried rice.

———

Origin Popular all over Indonesia
Chilli heat Mild
Serves 4 as a side

———

4 corn-on-the-cob
Sunflower oil, for the corn
Sea salt, to taste
Lime juice, to taste

For the chilli butter
40g unsalted butter, softened
½ long red chilli, finely chopped
1–2 tsp palm sugar or brown sugar, to taste
½ tsp sea salt
Drizzle of kecap manis (p.254)

Pull back the outer husks of the corn and remove any threads. Combine all the ingredients for the chilli butter in a small bowl and set aside.

Heat a griddle or large frying pan over a high heat or light a barbecue. Rub the corn with oil and salt and cook on the hot griddle or pan or over hot coals. As it is cooking, turn the corn every 2–3 minutes so that it chars all over. Alternatively, if you have a blowtorch, char the corn by placing it on a baking tray and letting the kernels turn black as you rotate the blowtorch around the cob.

Once the corn is sufficiently charred, baste with the soft chilli butter using a pastry brush. Remove the corn from the heat and baste again with more of the chilli butter. Transfer to a serving platter and baste with chilli butter once more, sprinkle with a final pinch of salt and squeeze over a generous amount of lime juice.

EGG AND SPRING ONION MARTABAK
MARTABAK TELUR

Culinary expert William Wongso took me to a food market in North Jakarta that specialises in the cuisine of Medan, which is where I first tried this dish. It is marvellous to watch the *martabak* chef at work: thin dough squares are laid on a wide hot plate and then furiously spread with an egg and spring onion mixture before being flipped with a giant spatula to cook the egg on both sides. The result is a crispy pancake sandwiched between two layers of delicious golden omelette.

My version uses a homemade *martabak* dough, which crisps up and bubbles as it pan-fries. If you're short of time, use spring roll wrappers or filo pastry squares as a substitute (the method for this variation follows the main recipe overleaf). It's best served immediately, with *sambal ulek* to dip, if you like.

Origin Medan, Sumatra
Chilli heat Mild
Serves 4 as a light main or 8 as a side

---

4 small banana shallots or 8 Thai shallots, peeled and thinly sliced
8 garlic cloves, peeled and thinly sliced
⅓ quantity of Martabak dough (p.256), rested for 2 hours
8 eggs, beaten
8 spring onions, thinly sliced on the diagonal
60g coriander, leaves and stalks finely chopped
Large pinch of sea salt
Coconut oil or sunflower oil, for frying
Lime wedges, to serve (optional)
1 quantity of Ground chilli sambal ulek (p.199), to serve (optional)
1 quantity of Cucumber, chilli and shallot pickle (p.88), to serve (optional)

Heat 2 tablespoons of oil in a frying pan over a medium heat. Add the shallots and garlic and fry until softened. Allow to cool.

Divide the martabak dough into four equal balls and cover with a clean tea towel to prevent them from drying out. Oil your hands and work surface. Take one ball of dough and flatten it as thin as you can with the palm of your hand. Using a rolling pin, roll the flattened ball into a thin sheet, about 1mm thick. Trim into a 15cm square. Lay the rolled-out martabak square on top of a sheet of baking parchment. Repeat with the remaining balls of dough. Place a piece of baking parchment between the rolled-out martabak sheets so they do not stick together.

Combine the eggs, spring onions, coriander and salt in a jug with the cooked shallots and garlic.

Heat 1 tablespoon of oil in a large frying pan wide enough to fit your martabak sheets, over a medium-high heat. Place a martabak sheet in the hot pan. Cook for 2–3 minutes or until bubbles form and the underside is a golden brown. Using tongs, turn the sheet over and cook on the other side for another 2–3 minutes. Flatten any air pockets with a spatula or fish slice. Pour some egg mixture on top, spreading it evenly with a spoon, ensuring there is enough to cover the sheet from corner to corner. If any egg spills onto the pan, push it back onto the martabak to keep it in a neat square.

After 2–3 minutes, carefully flip the martabak. Cover the other side with the egg mixture and leave for a further 2–3 minutes, then flip it over again to cook the other side. Once both sides are cooked through, transfer to a chopping board.

Continues overleaf

Repeat with the remaining martabak sheets and egg mixture.

Cut the cooked martabak into squares and serve immediately with lime wedges and sambal to dip, if using.

▬▬▬

Variation: Egg and spring onion martabak with spring roll wrappers or filo pastry

Substitute the martabak dough with 8 spring roll wrappers (measuring 15cm square) or 8 sheets of filo pastry cut into 15cm squares. If you can't find 15cm spring roll wrappers, cut a larger wrapper to size, or simply use larger wrappers and make a smaller quantity.

Make the egg mixture as per the main recipe. Heat 1 tablespoon of oil in a large frying pan over a medium-high heat, wide enough to fit the spring roll wrappers or filo pastry squares. Place a square in the pan, then brush the top of the sheet with oil or melted butter. Place a second square on top of the first and brush again with more oil or melted butter. When golden on the underside, which takes a couple of minutes, flip the squares over and cook on the other side until golden. Pour the egg mixture onto the square and continue to cook following the instructions in the main recipe.

LAMB MARTABAK
MARTABAK DAGING

This *martabak* is one of my favourite snacks to eat. With coriander- and cumin-spiced lamb encased in pastry, it's Indonesia's answer to a Cornish pasty. The traditional version is made with a thin, translucent sheet of oiled homemade dough that is pan-fried in a cast-iron pan (which I have included as a variation overleaf), but for easy entertaining, I wholly recommend using spring roll wrappers.

Lamb *martabak* is a fantastic canapé or appetiser to kick-start a dinner party. The filling can also be used to make a *martabak* filo pastry oven-baked pie (see the variation overleaf). Best eaten immediately and served with sambal on the side for dipping.

Origin Popular all over Indonesia
Sambal suggestion Caramelised shallot sambal
    bawang (p.200)
Makes 30 pieces

30 spring roll wrappers, 15cm square
1 banana or 1 beaten egg, for sealing
Coconut oil or sunflower oil, for pan-frying
Sunflower oil, for deep-frying

For the filling
450g lamb mince
2 garlic cloves, peeled and crushed
2 small banana shallots or 4 Thai shallots, peeled
    and finely chopped
8cm piece of ginger (about 40g), peeled and
    finely chopped
2 spring onions, finely chopped
½ bunch of chives, finely chopped
1 tsp ground coriander
½ tsp ground cumin
½ tsp sea salt
¼ tsp ground black pepper

Combine all the ingredients for the filling in a bowl and mix well. Heat 1–2 tablespoons of oil in a large frying pan over a medium-high heat, add the lamb filling and cook, stirring, until it is cooked through. Taste and adjust the seasoning as needed. Transfer to a bowl and allow to cool.

Line a tray with baking parchment. Place one spring roll wrapper on a chopping board, storing any unused wrappers under a clean tea towel so they do not dry out. Spread 1–2 tablespoons of the filling over one half of the wrapper, leaving a 1cm border. Cut a thick slice of the banana with the skin on and rub the banana flesh over the edges of the wrapper to help seal the skin together (if you prefer, you can brush with beaten egg). Fold the other half of the wrapper over the filling and press all the edges down. Place on the tray. Repeat until all the filling has been used up.

Fill a deep saucepan one-third full with sunflower oil and heat to 160°C. (If you do not have a kitchen thermometer, check the oil is at temperature by adding a cube of bread; it should turn golden in 25–30 seconds.) Fry the martabak in batches for 2–3 minutes until golden. Transfer to a tray lined with paper towels to absorb any excess oil.

Cut the martabak in half so the filling can be seen, then serve.

Variation: Vegan martabak

If you want to make the recipe vegan, replace the lamb with 225g potato and 225g butternut squash. Peel them both, removing the seeds of the butternut squash, and cut into 5mm cubes. Preheat the oven to 220°C/200°C fan/gas 7. Place on a flat baking tray, drizzle all over with oil, and

Continues overleaf

season with salt. Place two garlic bulb halves on the tray to add flavour. Bake in the oven for 15 minutes or until cooked through. Meanwhile, cook the remaining filling ingredients with 1 tablespoon of oil in a frying pan over a medium heat until softened, then stir through the roasted squash and potato.

Fill the spring roll wrappers, then cook and serve them as described in the main recipe.

Variation: Pan-fried martabak

Preheat the oven to 200ºC/180ºC fan/gas 6. Heat 3 tablespoons of oil in a large pan over a medium-high heat. When the oil is hot, gently place the martabak in the oil, cooking in batches so as not to overcrowd the pan. Continue turning in the oil until they are golden all over, about 5 minutes, adding more oil if necessary. Place on a tray lined with paper towels to absorb any excess oil, then transfer to a baking tray lined with baking parchment and finish cooking in the oven for 7–10 minutes.

Variation: Oven-baked martabak pie

If you prefer to bake rather than fry the martabak, substitute the spring roll wrappers with ready-made filo pastry (fresh or frozen). This version of martabak is baked as a rectangular pie, so you will need an oiled large, flat baking sheet. Make the filling following the main recipe. Preheat the oven to 200ºC/180ºC fan/gas 6. Place the filo pastry sheets on a work surface and cover with a clean, damp cloth to prevent the pastry from drying out. Using a sharp knife, trim 5 sheets so they are just smaller than your baking sheet. Place a sheet of filo pastry on the baking sheet and brush with oil or melted butter, and repeat with four more filo layers, brushing oil or butter

on every sheet. Spread the filling on top of the pastry, leaving a 3cm border around the edges. Fold the 4 edges into the middle to enclose the filling. Trim 5 more sheets of filo to match the size of the folded-in base. Place one of the trimmed sheets on top, brushing it with oil or butter, then repeat with the remaining layers. Bake for 45–50 minutes or until the filo pastry is deep golden brown. To serve, carefully transfer the martabak to a chopping board and cut into 5cm squares.

Variation: Martabak with homemade dough

Take 1 quantity of Martabak dough (p.256), divide and roll into 12 equal balls, then cover with a clean tea towel to prevent them from drying out. Oil your hands and work surface and flatten one of the balls of dough as thin as you can with the palm of your hand. Using a rolling pin, roll the ball into a thin 15cm square, about 1mm thick, trimming the edges. Place a piece of baking parchment between each square so they do not stick together. Repeat with the remaining dough, re-forming any trimmed offcuts to make more sheets.

Following the main recipe method, use the rolled-out squares in place of spring roll wrappers, using any filling you like, and brushing with an egg wash around the edges. Fold and seal the edges by pinching with your fingers. Cook following the main recipe instructions and cut in half into squares to serve. This should yield at least 24 bite-sized squares. Serve immediately.

BORNEO PORK AND PRAWN DUMPLINGS
CHAI KUE

The influence of Chinese cuisine is evident all over the city of Pontianak, Kalimantan, which sits on the island of Borneo. The dish that locals cannot live without is *chai kue* dumplings. Dumpling wrappers are simply folded in half over the filling – an easy process that anyone can master – to make half-moon shapes, which are then steamed, grilled or fried. What makes these dumplings especially delicious is the finishing sprinkling of garlic oil and fried garlic.

Chai kue come in a variety of flavours, but my favourite is this version with both pork and prawns. There is an equally satisfying vegan version with sweet potato (see overleaf). You can make your own dumpling dough or seek out gyoza and dumpling wrappers in the freezer section of Asian supermarkets. The wrappers defrost in the fridge in a couple of hours, but use them quickly as they become sticky when left defrosted for too long.

Pictured overleaf

――――

Origin Pontianak, Kalimantan (Borneo)
Chilli heat Mild
Makes About 25

――――

25 gyoza or dumpling wrappers, defrosted or
  1 quantity of Dumpling dough (p.257)
Sunflower oil, for frying

For the filling
250g raw prawns, peeled, deveined and finely
  chopped
125g minced pork
2 spring onions, very finely chopped
6cm piece of ginger (about 30g), peeled and grated
2 garlic cloves, peeled and crushed
Small handful of shiitake, chestnut or brown
  mushrooms, stems removed, finely chopped

Handful of coriander leaves or Chinese celery
  leaves, finely chopped
Pinch each of white and black pepper
Pinch of sea salt
2–3 tsp light soy sauce

To serve
Handful of Fried garlic (p.251)
Drizzle of the reserved fried garlic cooking oil
  (or sesame oil)
1 quantity of Soy, garlic and chilli dipping
  sauce (p.198)

――――

You will need a large frying pan with a lid.

Combine all the ingredients for the filling in a mixing bowl, bringing everything together with your hands until well combined. Heat a little oil in a frying pan over a medium-high heat. Take a teaspoon of the filling and make a small patty. Fry the patty in the pan until it is cooked through, allow to cool slightly and taste to check the seasoning. Adjust with salt, pepper and light soy sauce as needed.

Fill a small bowl with cold water and place it beside a chopping board. Lay a wrapper on the board and place a teaspoon of the filling in the centre. Don't be tempted to overfill the dumplings as they may burst open while cooking. Dab the edges of the wrapper with a little water and then fold it in half over the filling, making a half-moon shape. Pinch the edges of the wrapper together firmly to seal. Place the sealed dumpling on a tray lined with baking parchment and cover with a clean tea towel to prevent drying out. Repeat with the rest of the filling and remaining wrappers.

Continues overleaf

If preparing the dumplings in advance, they are best stored in the freezer. (They dislike being kept in the fridge for longer than an hour and dry out when left on the kitchen counter.) Lay the dumplings on a flat tray so they are not touching each other, then freeze for 4–5 hours. Once frozen, you can pop them all in a freezer bag or container.

The cooking method is the same whether using shop-bought wrappers or homemade dumpling dough. Heat 2 tablespoons of oil in a large frying pan over a medium-high heat. Place 10–12 dumplings in the pan and fry for 1–2 minutes on each side, or until crispy and golden. Add 2 tablespoons of cold water to the pan (taking care as the oil will start to spit) and immediately place a tight-fitting lid on top. Leave the dumplings to steam for 2–3 minutes, then remove the lid so the remaining water evaporates and the base of each dumpling crisps up again. If cooking from frozen, fry the dumplings on both sides until crispy and golden as above, but add 100ml cold water to the pan, cover and then steam for 4–5 minutes. Remove the lid and allow the remaining water to evaporate, then serve.

Cook the remaining dumplings in the same way and serve immediately with fried garlic slices, a drizzle of garlic oil or sesame oil, and the soy dipping sauce on the side.

——

Variation: Potato and sweet potato dumplings

For a vegan alternative, replace the prawns and pork mince with 200g each of potato and sweet potato (just like the traditional vegetable version of the dumpling served in Pontianak). Preheat the oven to 220ºC/200ºC fan/gas 7. Peel the potato and sweet potato and cut them into 5mm cubes. Cut a whole garlic bulb in half. Place the diced potato and sweet potato on a flat baking tray, drizzle all over with sunflower oil and season with salt. Place the garlic bulb halves on either side of the tray. Roast in the hot oven for 15 minutes or until cooked through. Meanwhile, fry the spring onions, ginger, garlic and mushrooms with 1 tablespoon of oil in a frying pan over a medium-high heat. Discard the roasted garlic and combine the roasted potato and sweet potato with the mushroom mixture. Season with the remaining ingredients and stir through the chopped coriander or celery leaf. Fill and cook the dumplings following the instructions in the main recipe, using vegan-friendly dumpling wrappers.

CHICKEN AND GARLIC SPRING ROLLS
LUMPIA AYAM SAYUR

A Chinese migrant first brought the spring roll to the markets of Semarang, central Java. Before long, locally sold spring rolls were spiced with the sweet and salty flavours of kecap manis, the syrupy soy sauce for which Indonesia is famous. They are now so popular that queues form every day at the busiest spring-roll vendors all over the country.

The spring rolls can be frozen in a single layer on a tray, then piled into a bag or container and kept in the freezer for up to 3 months. If cooking from frozen, cook for 6–7 minutes, or until golden. Once cooked they last for up to 2 days in the fridge and can be reheated in the oven for 10 minutes at 170°C/150°C fan/gas 3.

Pictured overleaf

Origin Semarang, Java
Chilli heat Mild
Makes About 12

———

75g dried rice vermicelli or other thin noodles
4 tbsp sunflower oil, plus extra for deep-frying
400g chicken mince, or pork mince if you prefer
100g shiitake, chestnut or brown mushrooms, stems removed, thinly sliced
2 carrots, peeled and grated
50g bean sprouts, roughly chopped
8 garlic cloves, peeled and thinly sliced
4 small spring onions, thinly sliced on the diagonal
3 tbsp kecap manis (p.254)
4½ tbsp oyster sauce
1 tbsp fish sauce
Juice of 1 lime
Pinch of sea salt
12 spring roll wrappers, 25cm square, defrosted if frozen
1 banana or 1 beaten egg, for sealing
1 quantity of Tomato sambal (p.194) or Soy, garlic and chilli dipping sauce (p.198), to serve (optional)

———

Place the noodles in a heatproof bowl and pour over boiling water. Leave to soak for 10 minutes (or follow the packet instructions). Once softened, drain and return to the bowl, tossing in a little oil to prevent them from sticking. Set aside.

Heat 2 tablespoons of oil in a frying pan over a high heat and add the mince. Stirring continuously, fry the mince until cooked through and well browned. Transfer to a bowl and set aside.

Heat another 2 tablespoons of oil in the pan over a medium-high heat, add the mushrooms and sauté for 2–3 minutes or until cooked through. Add the carrots and bean sprouts and stir for

1 minute, then add the garlic and cook for a further 1 minute. Return the cooked mince to the pan along with the noodles and spring onions, stirring for a further 1 minute. Finally, add the kecap manis, oyster sauce, fish sauce and lime juice, then continue to cook for a further 2 minutes or until the sauce is clinging to the meat. Taste and adjust the seasoning if necessary. (It is better for the filling to taste fairly strong at this stage because the spring roll wrapper absorbs a lot of the flavour during cooking.) Set aside to cool.

Lay a clean tea towel over the spring roll wrappers to prevent them from drying out. Line a tray with baking parchment. Cut a chunk of banana with the skin on to use as glue for the spring roll. (Alternatively, you can use beaten egg.) Peel one wrapper off the top of the pile and lay it on a chopping board, facing you like a diamond. Place 1–2 tablespoons of the filling on the bottom third of the wrapper. Roll the bottom corner of the wrapper up over the filling and then continue rolling until you reach the middle. Fold in the left and right corners, then rub the flesh of the banana along the edges of the exposed top corner of the wrapper. (If using beaten egg, brush this on instead.) Finish rolling up the rest of the wrapper and seal the final corner. Place the spring roll on the tray. Repeat with more wrappers until all the filling is used up.

Fill a deep saucepan one-third full with oil. Heat the oil to 160°C. (If you do not have a kitchen thermometer, check the oil is at temperature by adding a cube of bread; it should turn golden in 25–30 seconds.)

Carefully lower 4–6 spring rolls into the hot oil, without overcrowding the pan. Deep-fry for 4–6 minutes or until golden all over. Transfer to a tray lined with paper towels to absorb any

excess oil. Repeat with the remaining spring rolls. Serve immediately, with sambal or dipping sauce, if you like.

Variation: Vegetable spring rolls

Omit the mince from the recipe and instead triple the quantity of carrots, shiitake and bean sprouts. The remaining ingredients should stay the same. If you want to make the recipe vegetarian, replace the oyster sauce and fish sauce with light soy sauce, adding a little at a time until you are happy with the flavour. Once added to the pan, simmer to reduce this extra soy sauce for a couple of minutes.

Variation: Pan-fried spring rolls

Preheat the oven to 200°C/180°C fan/gas 6. Heat 3 tablespoons of oil in a large pan over a medium-high heat. Gently place the prepared spring rolls in the hot oil, cooking in batches so as not to overcrowd the pan. Continue turning the spring rolls in the hot oil until they are golden all over, about 5 minutes, adding more oil if necessary. Transfer to a tray lined with paper towels to absorb any excess oil, then to a baking tray lined with baking parchment, and finish cooking in the oven for 7–10 minutes.

LAMB AND POTATO CROQUETTES
KROKET KAMBING

These lamb and potato croquettes are a beloved snack for many Indonesians, the fusion of familiar flavours with Dutch cooking techniques from colonial times. A common street-food snack, they can be found all over the archipelago in bread shops and night food markets. They can be frozen in a single layer on a baking tray, then piled into a bag or container and kept in the freezer for up to 3 months. If cooking from frozen, increase the cooking time to 7–8 minutes. Once cooked, they last for up to 2 days in the fridge and can be reheated in the oven for 10 minutes at 170°C/ 150°C fan/gas 3.

Indonesian croquettes are not complete without the red and green bird's eye chillies that adorn them when served. I love to eat both the croquette and chilli garnish in a single mouthful, but my chilli tolerance is higher than most, so you can always remove them before eating or add just the smallest of chilli tails before serving.

Pictured overleaf

Origin Popular all over Indonesia

Chilli heat None (hot when eaten with the chilli garnish)

Makes 28

———

250g plain flour, seasoned with sea salt and white pepper

6 eggs, beaten

200g dried breadcrumbs

Sunflower oil, for deep-frying

Green and red bird's eye chillies, to garnish

1 quantity of Tomato sambal (p.194), to serve (optional)

For the mashed potatoes

1.4kg floury potatoes (such as Maris Piper), peeled and chopped into chunks

120g unsalted butter

Generous splash of whole milk

Sea salt and white pepper, to taste

For the filling

400g lamb mince

4 garlic cloves, peeled and finely chopped

16cm piece of ginger (about 80g), peeled and finely chopped

4 spring onions, finely chopped

2 tbsp kecap manis (p.254)

2 tbsp oyster sauce

2 tsp ground coriander

1 tsp sea salt

½ tsp ground black pepper

Place the potatoes in a large saucepan filled with salted cold water. Bring to the boil, then lower the heat to a medium simmer and cook for about 15–20 minutes or until easily pierced with the tip of a knife. Drain the potatoes and return them to the hot pan for a minute or so to dry out. You want a fine texture, so pass the potatoes through a ricer or mash them until smooth. Set aside.

In another pan, gently melt the butter with the milk. Add the warm mashed potatoes, stirring well. Season generously and allow to cool slightly before chilling in the fridge until firm.

Combine all the ingredients for the filling together in a mixing bowl. Heat a little oil in a large frying pan over a high heat. Add the filling mixture to the pan and fry, stirring continuously, until cooked through and well browned. Transfer to a clean bowl and allow to cool.

Line a tray with baking parchment. To make the croquettes, take 1½ tablespoons of the potato mash and flatten it in your hand to make a disc. Take a scant tablespoon of the filling and place it in the centre of the potato disc. Wrap the mash around the filling to make an oblong shape and pinch the edges to seal it together. The croquettes should be about 3–4cm wide and 6cm long. Place on the tray. Repeat with the remaining mashed potato and filling.

To coat, dip the croquettes first into the seasoned flour, shaking off any excess, then into the beaten egg and finally into the breadcrumbs. Return to the tray.

Fill a deep saucepan one-third full with oil. Heat the oil to 180ºC. (If you do not have a kitchen thermometer, check the oil is at temperature by adding a cube of bread; it should turn golden in 15 seconds.) Carefully lower 6–8 croquettes into the hot oil, making sure you don't overcrowd the pan. Deep-fry for 4–5 minutes or until golden all over. Transfer to a tray lined with paper towels to absorb any excess oil. Repeat with the remaining croquettes.

Slice the stalks off the bird's eye chillies. Make a hole in one end of each croquette using a chopstick or skewer and insert a chilli so the tail sticks out. Serve immediately with the sambal to dip, if using.

—

Variation: Vegetarian croquettes

Replace the mince with 800g of vegetables, such as peas, small cubes of butternut squash or mushrooms. (The total weight of vegetables will reduce once cooked.) Cook the vegetables along with the other filling ingredients, replacing the oyster sauce with light soy sauce, adding a little at a time until the flavour is just right. Fill and cook the croquettes following instructions in the main recipe.

Variation: Pan-fried croquettes

Preheat the oven to 200ºC/180ºC fan/gas 6. Heat 4 tablespoons of oil in a large frying pan over a high heat. When the oil is shimmering, gently place the croquettes in the oil, cooking in batches so as not to overcrowd the pan. Continue turning in the oil until they are golden all over, about 6–8 minutes, adding more oil if needed. Place on a tray lined with paper towels to absorb any excess oil, then transfer to a baking tray lined with baking parchment and finish cooking in the oven for 10 minutes.

SOUPS & RICE

—

Indonesians start each day with a hearty meal, and it typically begins with a rice dish or a noodle-laden soup. Breakfasts – such as creamy *bubur ayam* (p.71), a white rice porridge that is simmered in a spiced broth and served with shredded chicken and a mix of spring onions, boiled egg, fried shallots and roasted peanuts – are set before dawn in readiness for the morning call to prayer. For the early morning commuter rush, restaurants that specialise in a single dish are bustling, every table filled with hungry diners taking their fill before the start of a busy day's work.

Each region boasts its own breakfast specialities; in East Java it is *soto ayam* (p.68), a chicken soup served with softened tomato chunks and fried shallots in a rich stock layered with turmeric, garlic, shallot and coriander. In Medan, Sumatra, the Chinese-influenced noodle soup of *mie udang* (p.62) is full bodied with an irresistible prawn broth that is similar to a bisque, and served with poached prawns and freshly made rice noodles. Then there's *bakso* (p.72), dense and springy beef meatballs simmered in a clear, flavourful beef broth served with noodles and vegetables, a street food dish found on nearly every corner, from the congested streets of Jakarta to small, remote villages in the Lesser Sunda islands around Komodo National Park.

These soups tell a personal history for many of the people who serve them, with recipes passed down through generations. While in Jakarta, I searched for the best *soto Betawi* in town. It's one of the few traditional Indonesian meals

that is cooked with dairy: a beautiful beef stock mixed with coconut milk and cow's milk, served with slow-cooked tomatoes, potatoes, *kerupuk* crackers and soft, gelatinous chunks of beef (p.74). In the midst of a busy road lined with stalls selling Indonesian tat and trinkets was an unassuming restaurant called Soto & Sop Kaki Sapi. Ten small stools sat beneath a counter in a tiny space decorated in cobalt blue and yellow. One of the four brothers serving customers behind the counter wielded his cleaver on a wooden board, removing juicy chunks of beef jowl, cheek and skin from a braised cow's head. Open for breakfast and lunch every day of the week, the business was started thirty years ago by their grandfather, whose culinary legacy has since passed to his son and grandsons. At home, the family wake at 2.00 a.m. to start the morning's cooking with the grinding of the spice paste that will marinate the cow's head. Afterwards, it is steamed for two hours and then simmered to become the rich stock I tasted that day. Such is the commitment of these restaurant vendors who dedicate their lives to perfecting their dishes, through which their family story is proudly told with every bite.

You would be hard pressed to visit Indonesia and not find a variation of *nasi goreng*, the nationally loved fried rice dish, on restaurant menus. Recipes vary depending on the region or home cook you speak to, but most start with rice stir-fried with a warming spice paste and a mix of vegetables, tofu or meat, all served with a crispy fried egg on top and *kerupuk* crackers on the side. *Nasi goreng* is eaten at all times of the day, including breakfast, and for many it is considered the greatest of comfort foods. I've included my two favourites: a chicken *nasi goreng* (p.77), which is spiced with turmeric, white pepper, caramelised shallots and kecap manis, and a vegetarian *nasi goreng* (p.80) stirred together with the zing of fresh lemongrass and ginger sambal.

For Indonesians, heartwarming comfort food is the happiest start to the day, usually served in unfussy settings on laminate tables with wobbly legs, and a plastic banner at the entrance that proclaims the restaurant's speciality. Locals taste their soup or rice dish first, then season it with the lime wedges, kecap manis and sambal that sit in brightly coloured plastic bowls at every table. Stirring in sambal and seasonings this way, just a little at a time, enhances the flavour of these dishes and is a practice worth following when making them in your own home. Traditionally eaten on the hottest of sweltering days, the comfort and nourishment these Indonesian broths and rice dishes provide also have that marvellous ability to warm you from head to toe – so they're perfect whatever the weather and whatever the time of day.

AUBERGINE AND MUSHROOM SOUP
SOP SAYUR

This is a versatile, delicious and nourishing broth that will work with any vegetables lurking in your fridge, but for me, aubergine, mushrooms, tomatoes and tenderstem broccoli is the perfect combination. The fresh coriander – which is rarely used in Indonesia, where coriander seeds are far more common – gives it a lovely freshness that balances with the lemongrass-infused spice paste, the sweet depth of kecap manis and the sharpness of vinegar. Serve with a side of *sambal ulek* to add a little fire, and the added crunch of *kerupuk* or prawn crackers.

Origin Popular all over Indonesia
Chilli heat Moderate
Sambal suggestion Ground chilli sambal ulek (p.199)
Serves 4

1 large aubergine, cut into bite-sized chunks (about 2cm)
150g shiitake mushrooms (or brown, chestnut or white mushrooms), stems removed, thinly sliced
10 cherry tomatoes, halved
800ml coconut milk
400ml good-quality vegetable stock (p.248)
100g tenderstem broccoli, cut into large chunks
100g dried rice vermicelli noodles, or other thin noodles
2–3 tbsp kecap manis (p.254)
1–2 tbsp rice vinegar or white wine vinegar
Sea salt, to taste
Coconut oil or sunflower oil, for frying
Kerupuk (p.28) or prawn crackers, to serve
Lime wedges, to serve

For the spice paste
Large bunch of coriander
4 garlic cloves, peeled and sliced
2 small banana shallots or 4 Thai shallots, peeled and sliced
4 long red chillies, half deseeded, all sliced
2cm piece of ginger (about 10g), peeled and sliced
1 lemongrass stalk, outer woody layers removed, thinly sliced
1 tsp ground coriander

Pick some of the coriander leaves from the stalks and set aside to use as a garnish. Place all the coriander stalks and remaining leaves, along with the other spice paste ingredients, in a food processor and blend to a smooth paste.

Heat 2 tablespoons of oil in a wide, deep saucepan or casserole dish over a medium heat and fry the spice paste until fragrant, about 10 minutes. Add the aubergine chunks and sliced mushrooms with another 1 tablespoon of oil and cook, stirring, for 2–3 minutes. As soon as they have started to soften, add the tomatoes, coconut milk and vegetable stock and bring to the boil, then reduce to a simmer for 30 minutes. Add the broccoli and simmer for a further 5 minutes.

Meanwhile, place the noodles in a heatproof bowl, pour over boiling water and leave for 10 minutes (or follow the packet instructions). Drain and toss with a little oil to prevent them sticking together.

When ready to serve, check the vegetables are soft and the aubergine is cooked through. Add the noodles to the soup and warm through. Season with kecap manis, vinegar and salt. Taste to check the seasoning, then serve immediately garnished with the reserved coriander leaves, and the crackers, lime wedges and sambal on the side.

MEDANESE PRAWN BISQUE WITH NOODLES
MIE UDANG MEDAN

In the heart of Medan, Sumatra, I tried the most famous version of *mie udang*, a rich broth flavoured with prawns, layered with the scent of kaffir lime leaves and lemongrass and served with homemade rice noodles and prawns. The restaurant belongs to Ibu Amei, who for 30 years has been perfecting her recipe for a broth so flavourful you would be forgiven for thinking you were eating a bisque from the heart of France. The Medanese love strong flavours, and in this city *mie udang* is eaten for breakfast, so it's not uncommon to find long queues of people outside Ibu Amei's doors waiting to take their morning fill.

Here is my take on her unforgettable soup, best eaten with fried shallots, limes and *sambal terasi*. The flat rice noodles can happily be replaced with other similar noodles. The broth will keep for up to 3 days in the fridge, but if you have already cooked the prawns, it is best eaten on the day.

Origin Medan, North Sumatra
Chilli heat Mild
Sambal suggestion Fermented shrimp sambal terasi (p.208)
Serves 4

---

1 tsp coriander seeds
1 tsp black peppercorns
600g raw king prawns
1.5l good-quality fish stock (p.249)
200g flat rice noodles, 5mm wide, or other similar-shaped noodles
100g fried, smoked or firm tofu, thinly sliced
2 baby pak choi or similar Asian greens, chopped into chunks
Lime juice, to taste
Sea salt, to taste
Coconut oil or sunflower oil, for frying

For the spice paste
4 large tomatoes, cut into wedges
1 fennel bulb, including stalks, tough roots removed, roughly chopped
4 small banana shallots or 8 Thai shallots, peeled and sliced
2 kaffir lime leaves (optional)
2 bay leaves
1 lemongrass stalk, bruised and tied in a knot

To serve
2 spring onions, thinly sliced on the diagonal
4 duck or hen's eggs, soft-boiled for 6 minutes, peeled and halved
1 long red chilli, thinly sliced on the diagonal (optional)
Handful of Fried shallots (p.251), optional
Handful of coriander leaves or Chinese celery leaves (optional)
Lime wedges

Place a dry frying pan over a medium heat and toast the coriander seeds and black peppercorns until fragrant, about 1–2 minutes. Set aside.

For the spice paste, blend the tomatoes, fennel and shallots together in a food processor. Heat 2 tablespoons of oil in a frying pan on a medium heat. Add the blended vegetables, the kaffir lime leaves, if using, the bay leaves and lemongrass and fry in the pan until fragrant, about 15 minutes. Set aside.

Leaving the tails intact, peel and devein the prawns. Set aside the heads and shells for the prawn stock.

Place a deep saucepan or cast-iron casserole dish over a medium-high heat and add 1 tablespoon

Continues overleaf

of oil. Add the reserved prawn heads and shells and cook until they start to turn red. As they fry, crush the shells and heads with a wooden spoon to extract as much flavour as possible. Once the shells smell lovely and toasted, add the fish stock, the spice paste and the toasted coriander seeds and peppercorns. Bring to the boil. Scrape the base of the pan to get all the prawn flavour into the liquid. Simmer for 30 minutes, skimming away any scum that rises to the surface every 5–10 minutes. Top up the liquid with 250ml water after the first skim.

Meanwhile, pour boiling water over the noodles and soak for 10 minutes (or follow the packet instructions). Drain, run under cold water until cool and then transfer to a bowl, stirring through a drizzle of oil to keep the noodles from sticking to each other.

If the tofu is wet, spread the slices in a single layer on top of several layers of paper towels, then cover with additional paper towels. Let the tofu stand for 15 minutes, pressing down occasionally to squeeze out any excess moisture.

After 30 minutes, strain the stock through a sieve, pushing as much of the liquid through as possible using the back of a wooden spoon or ladle. Return the strained liquid to the pan and reduce over a high heat until the flavour is more concentrated, about 10 minutes. Taste and season with salt and lime juice as necessary.

Just before serving, poach the prawns in the broth on a gentle simmer for 3–4 minutes, until the prawns have changed colour, are opaque and curl up. While the prawns are cooking, add the noodles, pak choi and tofu to the broth to heat through.

Divide the soup between four bowls and top with your desired garnishes. Encourage your guests to squeeze the lime into the broth, to add a final kick of flavour.

WOKU MONKFISH STEW
IKAN WOKU BLANGA

Woku is a *bumbu* (spice paste) of Manado in North Sulawesi, an area famed for its love of chilli. The most impressive aspect of the region's food is the balance between spice and freshness. In *woku*, the heat of chilli is harmonised with tomatoes and lemon basil (a citrusy herb that can be substituted with Thai or Italian basil).

All kinds of meat and seafood can be made as a *woku* dish, but one of the most famous is *ikan woku blanga*, a fish stew. It's traditionally served with large chunks of fish on the bone, giving diners the opportunity to nibble the flesh off the bones as they are eating, a practice that Indonesians really enjoy, but my take on it uses succulent, boneless chunks of monkfish. You can use any white-fleshed fish with a firm, meaty texture such as cod or hake. Use a good-quality stock and serve with *sambal terasi* and *kerupuk* or prawn crackers.

———

Origin Manado, Sulawesi
Chilli heat Hot
Sambal suggestion Fermented shrimp sambal terasi (p.208)
Serves 4

———

2 lemongrass stalks, bruised and tied in a knot
2 kaffir lime leaves (optional)
400ml coconut milk
800ml good-quality fish stock (p.249)
2 large potatoes, cut into 2.5cm chunks
16 cherry tomatoes, halved
900g boneless monkfish or other firm white fish, cut into bite-sized chunks
3 spring onions, thinly sliced on the diagonal
Large bunch of lemon basil, Thai basil or Italian basil, leaves picked
Zest and juice of 2 limes, plus 1 lime for seasoning
Sea salt and white pepper, to taste
Coconut oil or sunflower oil, for frying
Kerupuk (p.28) or prawn crackers, to serve

For the spice paste
6 small banana shallots or 12 Thai shallots, peeled and sliced
14 garlic cloves, peeled and sliced
10cm piece of ginger (about 50g), peeled and sliced
2cm piece of fresh turmeric (about 10g), peeled and sliced (or ½ tsp ground turmeric)
2 tomatoes, quartered (or 12 cherry tomatoes, halved)
16 long red chillies, sliced

———

Place the spice paste ingredients in a food processor and blend to a fine paste.

Heat 4 tablespoons of oil in a deep saucepan over a medium heat, add the spice paste, lemongrass and kaffir lime leaves, if using, and cook until fragrant, about 10–15 minutes. Add 200ml of the coconut milk and cook for 10 minutes more.

Add the remaining coconut milk, fish stock, potatoes and tomatoes to the pan and bring to the boil, then reduce the heat and cook for 30 minutes. Reduce the heat to a very gentle simmer, add the fish and poach until cooked, about 5 minutes. Reserving a little for the garnish, add the spring onions and basil leaves, then the lime zest and juice. Season with salt, white pepper and more lime juice, if needed. Divide between four bowls and serve with a sprinkling of the spring onions and basil leaves, and crackers on the side if you like.

TIMORESE FISH SOUP
SOP IKAN TIMOR

This spectacular fish soup is a family recipe that, whenever I make it, fills my kitchen with the gorgeous aromas of lemongrass, ginger and lime. Taught to me by my aunty Kristina, the original dish is seasoned with *belimbing* (tiny, sour starfruit native to Indonesia) that she picks from her neighbour's tree. Recreating the dish in my London kitchen, I found segments of fresh lime to be an equally tart and delicious substitute.

I recommend using a meaty fish, such as monkfish or hake, which holds together nicely when poached in soups and suits the bold, spicy flavours of Indonesian cuisine. Eat with *kerupuk* or prawn crackers and a little *sambal terasi* on the side.

———

Origin Kupang, Timor
Chilli heat Mild
Sambal suggestion Fermented shrimp sambal terasi (p.208)
Serves 4

———

4 dried whole red chillies
2 kaffir lime leaves (optional)
2 limes, plus 2–3 extra for seasoning
1.2l good-quality fish or vegetable stock (pp.248–9)
4 ripe tomatoes, each cut into 6 wedges
900g boneless, firm white fish fillets such as monkfish, hake or cod, cut into bite-sized chunks
Large bunch of lemon basil, Thai basil or Italian basil, leaves picked
Sea salt, to taste
Palm sugar or brown sugar, to taste
Coconut oil or sunflower oil, for frying
Kerupuk (p.28) or prawn crackers, to serve

For the spice paste
4 lemongrass stalks, woody outer layers removed, thinly sliced
8cm piece of ginger (about 40g), peeled and sliced
8 small banana shallots or 16 Thai shallots, peeled and sliced
12 garlic cloves, peeled and sliced
4cm piece of fresh turmeric (about 20g), peeled and sliced (or 1 tsp ground turmeric)

———

Place the spice paste ingredients in a food processor and blend to a smooth paste.

Heat 4 tablespoons of oil in a deep saucepan over a medium heat and fry the spice paste with the dried chillies and kaffir lime leaves until fragrant, about 10–15 minutes.

Meanwhile, segment the limes: cut the tops and bottoms off so they sit flat on a chopping board. Using a sharp knife or a vegetable peeler, remove the skin and white pith from the fruit, so only the segments remain. Holding each lime over a bowl to catch any excess juice, very carefully cut along either side of the white membranes that hold the lime segments to release them. Set aside the bowl of lime juice.

Add the stock, tomato wedges and lime segments to the pan and simmer for 10 minutes. Reduce the heat to low and add the fish, poaching gently until it is cooked through. This should take about 5 minutes, depending on the thickness of the fish.

Once the fish is cooked, add the basil leaves, then season with salt, sugar, the extra limes and the reserved lime juice. Serve immediately, with crackers on the side, if you like.

AROMATIC CHICKEN NOODLE SOTO
SOTO AYAM

The Indonesian Ministry of Tourism declared *soto* to be one of five national dishes. Available all over the archipelago, from the west coast of Sumatra to the east in Papua, each region has its own interpretation of the national dish. Personally, I can't resist a bowl of *soto ayam*, a richly flavoured chicken bone broth with hundreds of variations, all with tender poached chicken and a hit of spice. I learnt this East Javanese version in Surabaya from Ibu Ley, a wonderful home cook who specialises in the district's cuisine. Her version is my firm favourite among the many I sampled. My take on her *soto* is hearty, nourishing and complex, with layers of cumin and coriander seeds in a golden turmeric-coloured broth that is incredibly delicious – a dish equally worthy of a special occasion or a Friday night in.

Indonesians love to eat *soto* with thinly sliced deep-fried potato *kerupuk*. I've given instructions on how to make these, but they can happily be substituted with a packet of ready salted or prawn cocktail crisps – the best kind of shortcut.

———

Origin Surabaya, Java
Chilli heat Mild
Sambal suggestion Fermented shrimp sambal terasi (p.208)
Serves 4

———

1 star anise
1 cinnamon stick
1 tsp black peppercorns
1 lemongrass stalk, bruised and tied in a knot
3 kaffir lime leaves (optional)
2 bay leaves
240g dried rice vermicelli noodles, or other thin noodles
1.6l good-quality chicken stock (p.250)

4 skinless, boneless chicken breasts
2 pak choi or similar Asian greens, chopped into large chunks
Handful of bean sprouts
Sea salt, to taste
Juice of 1 lime, to taste
Sunflower oil, for frying

For the spice paste
5cm piece of ginger (about 25g), peeled and sliced
4 garlic cloves, peeled and sliced
3 small banana shallots or 6 Thai shallots, peeled and sliced
½ tsp ground white pepper
½ tsp ground black pepper
½ tsp ground cumin
2 tsp ground coriander
2cm piece of fresh turmeric (about 10g), peeled and sliced (or ½ tsp ground turmeric)

To serve
4 eggs, soft-boiled for 6 minutes, halved
2 spring onions, thinly sliced on the diagonal (optional)
1 long red chilli, finely chopped (optional)
Handful of Fried shallots (p.251), optional
2 limes, cut into wedges or slices
A packet of ready salted or prawn cocktail crisps (if not making homemade kerupuk)

For the homemade potato kerupuk (optional)
5 baby potatoes, very thinly sliced

———

Warm a dry frying pan over a medium heat and toast the star anise, cinnamon stick and black peppercorns until fragrant, about 1–2 minutes. Remove from the pan and set aside.

Continues overleaf

Place the spice paste ingredients in a small food processor and blend to a smooth paste. If needed, add a splash of water to help it blend. Heat 2 tablespoons of oil in the frying pan over a medium heat and fry the spice paste with the lemongrass, kaffir lime leaves, if using, and bay leaves until softened and fragrant, about 10 minutes.

Meanwhile, place the noodles in a heatproof bowl, pour over boiling water and leave for 10 minutes (or follow the packet instructions). Drain well and toss with a little oil to stop the noodles sticking together.

Pour the stock into a deep saucepan and add the fried spice paste and toasted star anise, cinnamon stick and peppercorns. Bring to the boil, then reduce the heat and simmer for 10 minutes.

Place the chicken breasts in the broth and poach on a gentle simmer until cooked through. Depending on the size of the chicken breasts, this will take anywhere between 10 and 15 minutes. To test if the chicken is cooked, remove one breast and cut it through the middle. The chicken is cooked if the juices run clear and the meat is fibrous inside, with no opaque pink flesh.

If you are making your own potato kerupuk, you can prepare these while the chicken is poaching. Wash the thin slices of potato a few times in water to remove any starch, and then dry very well with several paper towels. Heat 150ml of oil in a deep saucepan to 130°C. (If you do not have a thermometer, check the oil is at temperature by adding a cube of bread; it should turn golden in 75 seconds.) Fry the crisps in batches until they are golden all over, then remove from the pan and drain on paper towels to remove any excess oil. Set aside.

When cooked, remove the chicken from the broth and, once cool enough to handle, shred into small pieces using a fork or your fingers. Cover the shredded chicken with foil and set aside. Reduce the broth over a high heat for 10 minutes to concentrate the flavour, then strain the broth through a sieve. Taste and season with salt and lime juice, if needed.

Return the shredded chicken to the broth along with the cooked noodles, pak choi and bean sprouts, and cook until warmed through. Divide the broth between four bowls and layer with your preferred garnishes. Serve with the kerupuk or potato crisps on top.

CHICKEN RICE CONGEE
BUBUR AYAM

Bubur ayam is a Chinese–Indonesian dish that consists of rice cooked slowly in a richly flavoured broth until it disintegrates and absorbs the liquid, becoming what Indonesians know as rice porridge or congee. I was often served silky, savoury and warming *bubur ayam* at breakfast. Choosing from the selection of toppings feels like being a child at an ice-cream parlour. You can add garnishes of fried tofu, shredded omelette, peanuts, fried shallot, chopped chilli and spring onions – experiment with toppings at home, using whatever you fancy.

I like to enhance the flavour of my broth by infusing it with aromatics placed inside a clean J-cloth or muslin tied up with string.

—

Origin Popular all over Indonesia
Chilli heat Mild
Sambal suggestion Caramelised shallot sambal bawang (p.200)
Serves 4

—

4 tsp coriander seeds
2 tsp black peppercorns
1 star anise
1 cinnamon stick
5cm piece of ginger (about 25g), peeled and thinly sliced
1.8l good-quality chicken stock (p.250)
4 skinless, bone-in chicken thighs
240g jasmine or basmati rice, rinsed until the water runs clear
1 lemongrass stalk, bruised and tied in a knot
4 banana shallots or 8 Thai shallots, peeled, roots removed, halved lengthways
2 kaffir lime leaves (optional)
2 bay leaves
4 dried whole red chillies
Sea salt, to taste

To serve
1 quantity of Egg crepes (p.252), rolled and thinly sliced
Small handful of unsalted roasted peanuts, roughly chopped
Small handful of Fried shallots (p.251)
2 spring onions, thinly sliced on the diagonal
1 long red chilli, thinly sliced
Lime wedges
Drizzle of light soy sauce or kecap manis (p.254)

—

Place the coriander seeds, peppercorns, star anise and cinnamon stick in a dry, deep saucepan over a medium heat and toast until fragrant, about 1–2 minutes. Place these toasted spices inside a clean J-cloth or muslin along with the sliced ginger and tie it up with string.

Pour the stock into the saucepan, add the tied-up spices and all the other ingredients for the congee, except the salt. Bring to the boil, then lower the heat and simmer for 1½ hours, removing the chicken thighs after 1 hour. Once cool enough to handle, shred the meat finely using a fork or your fingers, and discard the bones.

Continue to simmer the congee for the remaining 30 minutes until the rice has broken down into a thick soup. The texture of congee is a matter of personal preference, so if you prefer the rice grains to be less broken down, then shorten the cooking time accordingly.

Before serving, remove the tied-up spices and season with salt, if needed. Return the shredded chicken to the congee to warm it through.

Divide the congee between four bowls and garnish with your chosen toppings.

SPICED MEATBALL SOUP
BAKSO

Famously known as Barack Obama's favourite Indonesian meal – from his childhood in Jakarta – *bakso* is a soup made with bouncy, chewy meatballs in a beautifully flavoured beef broth. I've tasted versions with melt-in-the-mouth slow-cooked cuts of meat, which adds another dimension, so I have included it in my recipe.

I learnt this recipe from one of the best *bakso* vendors in Jakarta, and my version of it has become one of my favourite soups to make. For me, the fun of *bakso* is in the seasoning, so try to serve it as the street-food vendors of Jakarta do, with kecap manis, sambal, white vinegar and *kerupuk* crackers.

Origin Jakarta, Java
Chilli heat Mild
Sambal suggestion Ground chilli sambal ulek (p.199)
Serves 6

For the broth
600g beef brisket, trimmed of any fat and cut into 3cm cubes
16 garlic cloves, peeled and bruised
8 banana shallots or 16 Thai shallots, peeled, roots removed, halved lengthways
800ml good-quality beef stock
1.6l good-quality chicken stock (p.250)
2 pak choi or similar Asian greens, cut into chunks
240g dried flat rice noodles, 5mm wide, cooked, drained and rinsed in cold water
2 spring onions, thinly sliced on the diagonal

For the meatballs
4 garlic cloves, peeled and crushed
4 small banana shallots or 8 Thai shallots, peeled and finely chopped
500g beef mince

2 spring onions, thinly sliced on the diagonal
½ tsp sea salt flakes
¼ tsp white pepper
3 tsp ground coriander
1 tsp ground cumin
2 tsp cornflour
Coconut oil or sunflower oil, for frying

To serve
1 long red chilli, thinly sliced
Small handful of Fried shallots (p.251)
Kecap manis (p.254)
Kerupuk (p.28) or prawn crackers
Rice vinegar or white wine vinegar

To make the broth, place the beef brisket in a large, deep saucepan along with the garlic and shallots. Pour both stocks into the pan and bring to the boil over a high heat. Lower the heat and simmer, uncovered, for 2 hours or until the stock has reduced by about half.

To make the meatballs, heat 2 tablespoons of oil in a frying pan over a medium heat. Add the garlic and shallots and cook until softened. Allow to cool. Place the beef mince in a food processor with the softened garlic and shallots and the remaining meatball ingredients and pulse to a fine paste. Take about 1 tablespoon of the mixture and roll it tightly into a ball. Repeat with the remaining mixture to make 24–30 meatballs.

When the broth has simmered, add the meatballs to the pan and bring to the boil, then lower the heat and simmer for 5 minutes, until they are cooked through. Finally, add the pak choi, noodles and spring onions to the broth and warm through.

Divide the broth between four bowls. Scatter over the chilli and shallots and serve with the kecap manis, sambal, crackers and vinegar on the side.

BETAWI BEEF AND COCONUT SOUP
SOTO BETAWI

Tender chunks of slow-cooked brisket swim in this rich beef broth mixed with an aromatic spice paste of white pepper, ginger, garlic and shallots and simmered in both cow's milk and coconut milk. This delicious soup is famous in Jakarta, the home of the Betawi people, and examples of it can be found at food stalls in many streets in the city that never sleeps. When traffic is at a constant standstill, these roadside stalls provide respite and comfort in the form of these caramel-coloured bowls of goodness, always served with a side of pickles and lime wedges, and preferably *sambal ulek,* which is exactly how I suggest you enjoy it. Best eaten within 3 days.

Origin Jakarta, Java
Chilli heat Mild
Sambal suggestion Ground chilli sambal ulek (p.199)
Serves 4

1.2kg beef brisket, trimmed of any fat and cut into 3cm cubes
2 lemongrass stalks, bruised and tied in a knot
2 bay leaves
1 tbsp tamarind paste (or 1 tbsp lime juice mixed with 1 tbsp brown sugar)
700ml coconut milk
200ml whole milk
3 medium potatoes, peeled and cut into bite-sized chunks
3 tomatoes, quartered
2 spring onions, thinly sliced on the diagonal
Lime juice, to taste
Sea salt and white pepper, to taste
Coconut oil or sunflower oil, for frying

For the spice paste
4 small banana shallots or 8 Thai shallots, peeled and sliced
4 garlic cloves, peeled and sliced
1 tsp ground white pepper
2 candlenuts or macadamia nuts (or 4 almonds or cashews), toasted for best flavour
2cm piece of ginger (about 10g), peeled and sliced

To serve
Lime wedges
Cucumber, chilli and shallot pickle (p.88), optional

Place the beef brisket in a deep saucepan with the lemongrass and bay leaves. Pour in 1.5l water, bring to the boil, then lower the heat and simmer for 1 hour, carefully skimming off any scum that rises to the surface.

Meanwhile, place all the spice paste ingredients in a small food processor and blend to a smooth paste. Heat 2 tablespoons of oil in a frying pan over a medium heat, add the spice paste and cook until fragrant, about 10–15 minutes.

After the brisket has simmered for 1 hour, add the tamarind paste, coconut milk and whole milk, along with the spice paste. Bring to the boil, then lower the heat and simmer for another hour or until the brisket is soft and tender. Add the potato chunks for the final 30 minutes of cooking, then add the tomatoes and spring onions for the last 10 minutes. Continue to simmer and reduce the broth until it is thick and full flavoured. Season to taste with the lime juice, salt and pepper.

When ready to serve, divide the broth between four bowls and serve with the lime wedges, pickle and sambal, if using.

FRIED SHALLOT AND COCONUT RICE
NASI UDUK

Nasi uduk is comfort food for the native Betawi people of Jakarta, a popular dish with commuters and one commonly found on roadside stalls at breakfast, lunch and dinner. Served on a bed of banana leaf with peanut sauce and shredded egg crepe, the rice is steamed in coconut milk infused with the fragrance of Indonesian bay leaf (known as *salam*), lemongrass, cinnamon bark and cloves. Fried shallots and shallot-infused oil are stirred through the finished rice, making it not only a gorgeous side, but a dish that can be eaten on its own as a light meal, just as the Betawi do.

Origin Jakarta, Java
Serves 4 as a side or light meal

240g jasmine or basmati rice
1 tbsp coconut oil or sunflower oil
½ tsp sea salt

For the cooking liquid
1 cinnamon stick
2 cloves
250ml coconut milk, plus extra for topping up
1 bay leaf
1 lemongrass stalk, bruised and tied in a knot
3cm piece of ginger (about 15g), peeled and thinly sliced
¼ freshly grated nutmeg (or ¼ tsp ground nutmeg)
2 kaffir lime leaves (optional)

To serve
Large handful of Fried shallots (p.251)
Drizzle of the reserved fried shallot cooking oil (or sesame oil)
Egg crepes, rolled and sliced (p.252), optional
Peanut sauce (p.204), optional

For the cooking liquid, place the cinnamon stick and cloves in a dry, deep saucepan over a medium heat and toast for 1–2 minutes, until fragrant. Add the coconut milk, 100ml water and the bay leaf, lemongrass, ginger, nutmeg and kaffir lime leaves, if using. Bring to a gentle simmer, then remove the pan from the heat and leave the aromatics to infuse for 30 minutes. Strain the liquid through a sieve into a measuring jug, topping up with extra coconut milk if necessary to reach 350ml.

Rinse the rice until the water runs clear. Clean the pan, grease the inside with oil, then add the rice, salt and infused coconut milk.

Place the pan over a medium heat and bring to a gentle boil, stirring once so the rice doesn't stick to the base of the pan. Turn the heat down to low, cover the pan with foil and place a lid on top. Simmer for 15 minutes, then remove from the heat. Leave for 10 minutes, covered, to finish off the cooking. When ready to serve, remove the lid and foil, then fluff the grains of rice with a fork.

To serve, stir a drizzle of the reserved shallot oil (or sesame oil) through the rice, then add a large handful of fried shallots and stir again. Season with more salt if needed. For the ultimate traditional Betawi meal, serve with sliced egg crepes and peanut sauce. Eat immediately.

CHICKEN NASI GORENG
NASI GORENG AYAM

I've been eating chicken fried rice for as long as I can recall and it's a dish of which I never tire. This version of *nasi goreng* is my absolute favourite. The galangal and white pepper give it a good amount of heat, which is balanced by the sweetness of the kecap manis and the saltiness of the soy and fish sauce. The fried duck egg with a runny yolk on top is sheer luxury. With the added crunch of green beans, fried shallots and *kerupuk* or prawn crackers, this dish hits all the right spots and is my favourite choice for a Friday night in.

Pictured overleaf

Origin Popular all over Indonesia
Chilli heat Mild
Sambal suggestion Peanut sauce (p.204)
Serves 2 as a large main or 4 as a side

---

2 skinless, boneless chicken thighs, cut into small, bite-sized cubes
2 garlic cloves, peeled and thinly sliced
8cm piece of galangal or ginger (about 40g), peeled and woody stem removed, finely chopped
1 small banana shallot or 2 Thai shallots, peeled and thinly sliced
Handful of green beans, chopped into small chunks
2 spring onions, chopped into large chunks
¼ tsp ground turmeric
95g jasmine or basmati rice, cooked and cooled (240g cooked weight)
2 tbsp kecap manis (p.254)
1½ tsp fish sauce
2 tsp light soy sauce
Sea salt and white pepper, to taste
Coconut oil or sunflower oil, for frying

To serve
2 duck or hen's eggs
1 tbsp Fried shallots (p.251)
½ long red chilli, thinly sliced
Kerupuk (p.28) or prawn crackers

Season the chicken pieces with salt and white pepper. Heat 1 tablespoon of oil in a large frying pan or wok over a high heat and fry the chicken until cooked through, about 3 minutes. Remove and set aside.

Add another tablespoon of oil to the pan, add the garlic, galangal or ginger and shallots and cook over a medium-high heat until fragrant. Add the green beans, spring onions and turmeric and cook for 1 minute.

Add the rice to the pan, breaking up any clumps with a wooden spoon. Ensure all the ingredients are well combined and the rice is warmed through. Return the chicken to the pan. Season with the kecap manis, fish sauce, light soy sauce and a large pinch of white pepper, and extra salt if needed.

Meanwhile, fry the eggs. Place a large non-stick frying pan over a medium-high heat and add 1 tablespoon of oil. Once shimmering, crack the eggs directly into the oil. Cook for 2–3 minutes until the whites are partially cooked. Tilt the pan and spoon the hot oil over the egg whites until they are fully cooked (I like my yolk runny, but cook yours to your liking). Season with salt.

Divide the fried rice between two serving plates and garnish with the fried shallots, sliced chilli and fried eggs on top. Serve with crackers.

VEGETABLE NASI GORENG
NASI GORENG SAYUR

The fresh zing of the Balinese lemongrass and ginger *sambal matah*, along with the aromatic flavour of the spice paste and the sumptuous addition of a fried duck egg, make this *nasi goreng sayur* a feast of texture and flavour. If you want to make it vegan, simply omit the fried egg. Serve with *kerupuk* or prawn crackers on the side.

——

Origin Bali
Chilli heat Hot
Serves 2 as a large main or 4 as a side

——

½ leek, thinly sliced
1 banana shallot or 2 Thai shallots, peeled and
     thinly sliced
1 long red chilli, thinly sliced
¼ tsp ground turmeric
1 pak choi or similar Asian green, cut into chunks
95g jasmine or basmati rice, cooked and cooled
     (240g cooked weight)
2 tbsp kecap manis (p.254)
1½ tbsp light soy sauce
1 tsp tomato purée
½ tsp rice vinegar or white wine vinegar
1 quantity of Fresh Balinese sambal matah (p.206)
Sea salt and white pepper, to taste
Coconut oil or sunflower oil, for frying

To serve
2 duck or hen's eggs
1 tbsp Fried shallots (p.251)
1 spring onion, thinly sliced on the diagonal
Kerupuk (p.28) or prawn crackers

Heat 2 tablespoons of oil in a large wok or frying pan over a medium heat. Add the sliced leek and shallots and cook for 5 minutes or until just softened. Add the chilli and turmeric and cook for a further 2 minutes, then add the pak choi and cook for 1 minute.

Add the rice to the pan, breaking up any clumps with a wooden spoon and ensuring that all the ingredients are well combined and the rice is warmed through. Add the kecap manis, soy sauce, tomato purée and vinegar to the rice and combine. Finally, stir through the sambal matah. Once everything is combined, remove from the heat and season with salt and pepper.

Meanwhile, fry the eggs. Place a large non-stick frying pan over a medium heat. Add 1 tablespoon of oil and, once shimmering, crack the eggs directly into the oil. Cook for 2–3 minutes until the whites are partially cooked. Tilt the pan and spoon the hot oil over the egg whites until they are fully cooked (I like my yolk runny, but cook yours to your liking). Season with salt.

Divide the fried rice between two serving plates and garnish with the fried shallots, sliced spring onion and the fried eggs on top. Serve with a side of crackers, if you like.

VEGETABLES, TOFU & TEMPEH

—

It's 6.00 a.m. at the market in Ubud, Bali. Woven baskets, plastic trays and tubs are filled with a kaleidoscope of fresh vegetables and fruit by sellers touting their wares. Hundreds of early risers arrive at the market as it opens before sunrise to choose the best produce for their daily cooking. Here are myriad traders – a sea of black hair and brightly patterned batik shirts – selling, sorting and buying. The market sellers are clever, offering peeled garlic cloves and shallots, freshly made coconut milk, and other pre-prepared produce that saves the buyer precious time in the kitchen. White, purple and black aubergines sit side by side, some of them small, others as long as a tuba. There are tomatoes, carrots and too many varieties of yam, sweet potato and cassava to count. Indonesians always buy their produce fresh on the day they plan to prepare it. It's a wonderful part of their tradition, a practice that reflects the great pride they take in making their dishes, and the ingredients that go into them, shine. Larger Western-style supermarkets exist and are popular for convenience – most traditional fresh food markets close by 11.00 a.m. – but for quality and freshness, most Indonesians still prefer to buy their groceries from retailers at the market.

Thanks to these thriving food markets, which are present in every village and town, vegetables are fresh, varied, accessible and affordable, and therefore take a central role at every mealtime. When meat commands a higher purchase price, vegetables take its place. Nearly every feast I attended featured a favoured vegetable side dish known as *kangkung* (p.100), made with the inexpensive

and abundantly available morning glory (water spinach) stir-fried with fragrant garlic, ginger, shallots and *terasi* – a mouthwatering dish to eat. Vegetables are also preserved as piquant pickles known as *acar* (pp.88–9), spiced with Indonesian flavours such as turmeric or chilli, or eaten raw tossed with grated coconut and deep-flavoured spice pastes in the *lawar* salads of Bali (p.94). Perhaps the most famous Indonesian vegetable dish, found on nearly every restaurant menu, is *gado-gado* (p.92), a cooked salad of mixed vegetables coated in a warm, creamy peanut sauce and served with *kerupuk* crackers. However it is prepared, a vegetable dish in Indonesia rises to new heights when combined with their distinctive spices and punchy seasonings, which make these healthy ingredients a delight to devour.

Like vegetables, tofu and tempeh form an important part of the Indonesian table, where they are transformed from bland protein into plant-based treasures. Tempeh is a fermented soybean cake, a cousin of the soy-based tofu but with a dense texture and earthy flavour, and is said to have many health benefits including lowering cholesterol and aiding digestion. In Indonesia, this versatile ingredient is used in many dishes and can be steamed, stir-fried, grilled, poached in broth to absorb maximum flavour, or fried until crisp and golden. The first use of tempeh was recorded in Java in the early eighteenth century, and today it is described as Indonesia's gift to the world. It's used for meat-free burger patties in international street-food markets, sold globally as a substitute for bacon, and is often the star of vegan buddha bowls served with chia seeds and other superfoods that were made famous in Bali and now have a home at brunch spots all over the world.

Vegetarian dishes are celebrated at the Indonesian dinner table. Flavours are amplified and textures vary from fried to steamed to poached to sautéed. A common meal of rice, sambal and *kerupuk* crackers will always be served with vegetables, tofu and tempeh and you should never feel the absence of meat. Eating vegetarian food in Indonesia is an enlightenment. Vegetables never stand alone, but are combined with the striking, bold flavours of Indonesia – the fragrance of lemongrass, the zest of kaffir lime, the quintessential spice pastes and the richness of coconut – to make them an essential part of the everyday diet of Indonesians.

CUCUMBER, CHILLI AND SHALLOT PICKLE
ACAR KETIMUN

This is a quick pickle that goes with nearly everything: rice, burgers, salads, fish and, of course, satay. My grandmother Popo used to carve carrots, cucumbers and an assortment of fresh vegetables into flowers and other beautiful shapes as she prepared her *acar* pickles. I've spared you the whittling work (although she found this highly relaxing), but the key to this fiery pickle is to cut your ingredients as finely as possible to soak up maximum flavour. Because the pickle is very thinly sliced, the cucumber turns grey after 1 day. It will keep for up to 3 days in the fridge, but when serving it to guests make it no more than 1 day in advance for optimal beauty.

Pictured with Egg and spring onion martabak, p.39

Origin Popular all over Indonesia
Chilli heat Hot
Serves 4 as a small side

―――

100ml rice vinegar or white wine vinegar
100g caster sugar
1–2 tsp sea salt, to taste
⅓ cucumber, skin on, halved lengthways
2 small banana shallots or 4 Thai shallots, peeled and very thinly sliced
1 long red chilli, thinly sliced on the diagonal (deseeded if you prefer less heat)

―――

To make the pickling liquid, mix the vinegar, sugar and salt in a bowl.

Slice the cucumber using a mandolin if you have one, or very thinly slice with a sharp knife. Add the sliced cucumber, shallots and chilli to the pickling liquid and stir together. Set aside for 1 hour for the ingredients to pickle.

Once ready to serve, drain the liquid from the pickle and serve as well-drained as possible.

TURMERIC PICKLE
ACAR KUNYIT

Indonesians eat a large, colourful spread of dishes at every meal, and the inclusion of a sharp pickle known as *acar* – alongside rice, sambal and *kerupuk* crackers – is always a welcome addition at the dinner table. I use cauliflower, carrot and mangetout in this wonderfully spiced turmeric pickle, but you can make it your own with any vegetables or fruits ranging from cabbage and mushrooms to pineapples and cucumber. This pickle will last for 1 month when stored in a sterilised jar in the fridge (although it never stays around for that long in my house). It benefits from being made 1 day in advance to absorb the spices, but it is also a fast-acting pickle that can be eaten as soon as it has cooled. You will need a 1-litre jar or two 500ml jars.

Pictured with Pickled sweet and sour coleslaw (overleaf)

———

Origin Popular all over Indonesia
Makes 1 litre

———

1½ tsp cumin seeds
2 tsp coriander seeds
1 cinnamon stick
8cm piece of fresh turmeric (about 40g), thinly
    sliced (or 2 tsp ground turmeric)
6 garlic cloves, peeled and thinly sliced
500ml rice vinegar or white wine vinegar
60g caster sugar
1½ tbsp sea salt
2 bay leaves
1 small or ½ large head of cauliflower (about 270g),
    cut into small, bite-sized florets
2 large carrots, peeled and cut into 4cm x 5mm
    batons
50g mangetout, halved
Coconut oil or sunflower oil, for frying

Place the cumin seeds, coriander seeds and cinnamon stick in a dry saucepan over a medium heat and toast until fragrant, about 1–2 minutes. Tip onto a plate and set aside.

Heat 1 tablespoon of oil in the pan over a medium heat and add the turmeric and garlic. Fry for 2–3 minutes to soften, but do not brown the garlic. Add 250ml water to the pan, along with the vinegar, sugar, salt and bay leaves. Bring to the boil, then reduce the heat and simmer for 7 minutes, stirring occasionally. Add the cauliflower florets, return to the boil and simmer for a further 3 minutes, then turn off the heat. Add the carrot batons, then after 5 minutes add the mangetout. Leave to cool.

Drain the vegetables, reserving the pickling liquid. Transfer the pickled vegetables to a sterilised jar, top up with the reserved pickling liquid and seal with the lid.

PICKLED SWEET AND SOUR COLESLAW
ASINAN SAYUR

This version of *asinan sayur* is my interpretation of the classic dish that hails from Jakarta and West Java. It is a pickled vegetable salad fragrant with cinnamon, coriander and cumin, which is served with peanut sauce or a sweet and sour dressing. My version opts for the latter, which gives the dish a complex flavour that is both piquant and fresh but, if you love this salad like I do, you can also try it with Peanut sauce (p.204).

Traditionally, Indonesians place the pickles with chopped-up fruit and vegetables in a serving bowl and cover it with the dressing so that it almost resembles a soup, but I prefer mine with a modest drizzle. Once the pickle, salad and dressing have been combined, this dish is best eaten on the day.

———

Origin Jakarta and West Java
Chilli heat Mild
Serves 2 as a light main or 4 as a side

———

For the dressing
1 tbsp coconut oil or sunflower oil
2 garlic cloves, peeled and finely chopped
1 long red chilli, finely chopped
1 tbsp caster sugar
¼ tsp sea salt
1 tbsp tamarind paste (or 1 tbsp lime juice mixed
    with 1 tbsp palm or brown sugar)

For the salad
100g firm or smoked tofu, cut into 1 x 3cm chunks
75g tenderstem broccoli
3 Chinese cabbage or red cabbage leaves, or
    a mixture of the two, finely shredded with the
    thickest parts discarded
50g unsalted roasted peanuts, roughly chopped
Handful of coriander or Chinese celery leaves
1 spring onion, thinly sliced on the diagonal

For the pickle
½ quantity of Turmeric pickle (p.89), drained
    of liquid

———

To make the dressing, heat the oil in a frying pan over a medium heat. Cook the garlic and chilli for 2–3 minutes until softened, then transfer to a mortar and pestle. Add the sugar, salt and tamarind paste to the mortar, then grind to a paste. Stir in 3 tablespoons of water to loosen the dressing. Set aside.

If the tofu is wet, spread the pieces in a single layer on top of several layers of paper towels, then cover with additional paper towels. Let the tofu stand for 15 minutes, pressing down occasionally to squeeze out any excess moisture.

Bring a saucepan of salted water to the boil, add the broccoli and cook for 1–2 minutes. Drain and refresh under cold running water until cool. Chop into large chunks, then set aside.

To serve, drain the pickle of its liquid. Toss the pickle with the pressed tofu, broccoli and shredded cabbage. Reserving a little of each for the garnish, stir through the roasted peanuts and coriander or celery leaves.

Pour the dressing over the salad and toss all the ingredients together. Transfer to serving plates and garnish with the spring onion, remaining peanuts and coriander or celery leaves, then serve immediately.

GADO-GADO SALAD WITH PEANUT SAUCE
GADO-GADO

There are many dishes served with peanut sauce in Indonesia, but none is more famous than *gado-gado*, which literally translates from Indonesian as 'mix-mix'. It also comes from the word *menggado*, which is to consume something without rice, a rarity on these islands. You can easily substitute the suggested vegetables with whatever you have to hand – the key to this dish is a good peanut sauce and a hefty helping of *kerupuk* or prawn crackers.

You can eat this dish on its own, but it also makes a great side dish as part of a larger feast. The peanut sauce will last for up to 5 days, but once tossed together, *gado-gado* is best eaten on the same day.

___

Origin Java
Chilli heat Mild
Serves 2 as a main or 4 as a side

___

60g fried, firm or smoked tofu, cut into bite-sized chunks
150g baby potatoes, halved
100g tenderstem broccoli
100g green beans, trimmed
60g tempeh, sliced into 1cm wide x 3cm long chunks (optional, or replace with more tofu)
Kecap manis (p.254), for grilling (optional)
2 quantities of Peanut sauce (p.204)
1 carrot, peeled and cut into long, thin matchsticks
75g bean sprouts
½ cucumber, sliced into thin rounds
16 cherry tomatoes, halved
4 eggs, hard-boiled for 10 minutes, halved
2 tbsp Fried shallots (p.251), optional
Sea salt, to taste
Coconut oil or sunflower oil, for frying
Kerupuk (p.28) or prawn crackers, to serve

If the tofu is wet, spread the pieces in a single layer on top of several layers of paper towels, then cover with additional paper towels. Let the tofu stand for 15 minutes, pressing down occasionally to squeeze out any excess moisture.

Bring a pan of salted water to the boil over a high heat and add the baby potatoes. Simmer for 5–8 minutes, until tender when pierced with a fork. Drain and allow to cool, then set aside.

Refill the pan with salted water, bring to the boil and blanch the broccoli and beans for 1–2 minutes until bright green, crisp and just cooked through. Drain and cool in cold water, then set aside.

Heat 4 tablespoons of oil with a large pinch of salt in a wok or frying pan over a high heat. When the oil is shimmering, add the tempeh and fry for 3–4 minutes until golden. Drain on a tray lined with paper towels. Alternatively, if you prefer to grill tempeh, brush it with a mixture of 1 tablespoon each of oil and kecap manis and place it under the grill on a high heat for 3–4 minutes each side.

Loosen the peanut sauce with water until it reaches a pourable consistency. Transfer the peanut sauce to a pan and place it over a low heat until just warmed through.

Arrange the baby potatoes, broccoli, beans, tofu, tempeh, carrot, bean sprouts, cucumber, tomatoes and eggs on individual serving plates or bowls. Sprinkle with the fried shallots and place the crackers on one side of the plate. Serve the peanut sauce on the side in a serving bowl or jug or drizzle generously over the top of each plate, as I like to do. Serve immediately.

BALINESE COCONUT LAWAR SALAD
LAWAR BUNCIS BALI

Lawar is a type of salad that hails from Bali, where it originated as a ceremonial dish – both as an offering and as a feast to be shared by the hundreds who visit the Hindu temples. There are many variations on the island, each with their own significant meaning. My vegan version is a beautiful salad full of texture and fragrant citrus flavours; you will see why it is a dish worthy of celebration.

———

Origin Bali
Chilli heat Moderate
Sambal suggestion Ground chilli sambal ulek (p.199) or Fresh Balinese sambal matah (p.206)
Serves 2 as a main or 4 as a side

———

1 long red chilli, deseeded and thinly sliced on the diagonal
180g green beans, trimmed and chopped into 1cm pieces
100g frozen podded edamame or broad beans
100g mangetout, cut into very thin matchsticks
2 kaffir lime leaves (optional), stems removed, very finely chopped
1 lemongrass stalk, outer woody layers removed, very finely chopped
60g unsweetened desiccated coconut
2 tbsp Fried shallots (p.251)
1 tbsp Fried garlic (p.251), or extra fried shallots
Handful of coriander leaves or Chinese celery leaves
Zest and juice of 2 kaffir limes or standard limes
Up to ¾ tsp palm sugar or brown sugar
Up to ¾ tsp sea salt
Coconut oil or sunflower oil, for frying

For the spice paste
6cm piece of ginger (about 30g), peeled and sliced
6cm piece of galangal (about 30g), woody stem removed, sliced (optional)
3 garlic cloves, peeled and thinly sliced
2 long red chillies, deseeded and sliced
2 small banana shallots or 4 Thai shallots, peeled and sliced
2 tsp ground coriander
1 tsp ground cumin
¼ tsp ground turmeric
¼ tsp ground nutmeg
¼ tsp sea salt
¼ tsp ground black pepper
¼ tsp ground white pepper

———

Place the spice paste ingredients in a small food processor and blend to a paste. Heat 2 tablespoons of oil in a frying pan over a medium heat and cook the spice paste for about 10 minutes until fragrant, making sure it doesn't burn. Remove and allow to cool.

Heat another tablespoon of oil in the frying pan over a medium heat and add the chilli with a pinch of salt. Cook until softened and set aside.

Bring a pan of salted water to the boil. Add the green beans and cook for 1–2 minutes until they are crisp, tender and bright green. Drain and refresh under cold running water. Set aside in a large bowl. Repeat with the edamame beans, cooking for 1–2 minutes. Once cool, add to the beans with the mangetout, kaffir lime leaves and lemongrass.

Mix the spice paste with the desiccated coconut, then stir it through the vegetables. Add the fried shallots, fried garlic and coriander or Chinese celery leaves and mix together. Add the fried chilli to taste, reserving some for garnish, and season to taste with the lime zest and juice, sugar and salt.

TIMORESE TOMATO AND CORIANDER SALAD
LAWAR TOMAT DAN TURIS

In Kupang, Timor, I was taken to my family's favourite restaurant, Depot Selera. Sitting inside a glass cabinet at the counter, their signature dishes fill multiple trays in a celebration of the local cuisine. It was here that I first tasted this Timorese tomato and coriander salad made with wild bush tomatoes that grow locally, picked and marinated in a lime vinaigrette to form this fresh salad that I adore. Here I've substituted sun-dried or sun-blushed tomatoes – just try to buy the best quality you can afford. Fresh raw salads do exist in Indonesia, but are less common than the more typical poached, steamed, boiled, stir-fried or fried vegetables. This beautiful salad can be eaten on its own or as a side with fish, chicken or satay.

Origin Kupang, Timor
Chilli heat Moderate
Serves 2 as a light meal or 4 as a side

———

70g frozen podded edamame beans or broad beans
60g coriander, leaves roughly chopped and stalks finely chopped
12 spring onions, thinly sliced on the diagonal
260g cherry tomatoes, halved
80g good-quality sun-dried or sun-blushed tomatoes
4 long red chillies, deseeded and thinly sliced
Zest and juice of 2 limes
4 tsp rice vinegar or white wine vinegar
Sea salt, to taste

———

Bring a pan of salted water to the boil over a high heat. Add the edamame or broad beans and cook for about 1 minute. Drain and run under cold water until cooled.

Combine the blanched beans with the coriander, spring onions, cherry tomatoes, sun-dried tomatoes, red chillies and lime zest in a bowl. Stir the vinegar and lime juice together in a small bowl. Pour the dressing over the salad, tossing until everything is well coated. Season with salt and serve immediately.

FRIED CHILLI CORN
JAGUNG GORENG

This is a special dish in my family, one that's simple to make in less than 15 minutes, and yet incredibly delicious. When my mother and father were married in 1975, they honeymooned in Indonesia. It was my mother's first time overseas and they explored Bali, Java and Timor at a time when those places were relatively untouched by the tourism Indonesia is so famous for today. When they reached Kupang, my grandmother Popo threw the newlyweds a second wedding celebration. It was the first time my mother had met my grandmother and extended family, and it was an exciting and overwhelming time. The people, the smells, the humidity and the flavours were all new to my mother, whose fair skin had burnt scarlet from a day riding around on my father's motorbike. She was not accustomed to the taste of chilli but it was Popo's *jagung goreng* that gave her a first introduction, one she remembers vividly from that trip. With only a hint of chilli among the corn, shallots, fish sauce and paprika flavours that ran through the dish, it's a meal she still requests whenever we visit Indonesia – a family recipe that is still cooked by my aunties to this day, and which I share with you here.

While you could use canned or frozen sweetcorn, the superior texture and flavour you get from fresh corn really is worth the extra effort. If you are using canned or frozen corn, however, squeeze out as much moisture from the kernels as possible – the easiest way is in between layers of paper towels. *Jagung goreng* will keep for up to 1 day in the fridge and is best served as a vegetable side.

Origin Kupang, Timor
Chilli heat Moderate
Serves 2 as a side

---

2 corn-on-the-cob or 175g canned or frozen sweetcorn kernels
4 small banana shallots or 8 Thai shallots, peeled and sliced
2 long red chillies, deseeded and thinly sliced (keep the seeds if you prefer more heat)
½ tsp paprika
1 tbsp fish sauce, or to taste
Coconut oil or sunflower oil, for frying

If using fresh corn, remove the outer husk and threads, then carefully slice down the outside of the cob with a knife, as close to the core as possible, to remove the kernels. Set them aside.

Heat 2 tablespoons of oil in a wok or a frying pan over a medium heat. Add the sliced shallots and cook, stirring, for 2–3 minutes until softened. Add the corn kernels, sliced chillies, paprika and fish sauce. Continue cooking for a few minutes until all of the ingredients are warmed through. Season with extra fish sauce or paprika, if needed.

SOY MUSHROOMS AND PAK CHOI
JAMUR SAYUR KECAP

This divine mushroom and pak choi stir-fry will pair well with any savoury dish in this book. Inspired by Indonesian flavours, but not belonging to any specific region, this umami-packed recipe is layered with garlic, light soy and a little vinegar to provide punchy, sharp flavours for a refreshing and balanced side dish.

Serves 4 as a side

—

2 tbsp light soy sauce

4 tsp palm sugar or brown sugar

4 garlic cloves, peeled and thinly sliced

300g shiitake mushrooms (or brown or oyster mushrooms), woody stems removed, thickly sliced or left whole if small and tender

Large pinch of sea salt

2 tbsp rice vinegar or white wine vinegar

2 pak choi (or similar Asian greens), chopped into small chunks

Coconut oil or sunflower oil, for frying

—

Mix the soy sauce with the sugar in a small bowl and set aside.

Heat 2 tablespoons of oil in a large frying pan or wok over a high heat. Add the garlic and cook for 1–2 minutes, stirring continuously. Add the mushrooms with the pinch of salt and cook for 3 minutes or until browned. Add the vinegar and continue to cook until the liquid has nearly evaporated. Add the pak choi and cook for a couple of minutes or until softened.

Finally, add the soy and sugar mixture and stir-fry for a further 2 minutes until the sauce has reduced and coated the ingredients. Serve immediately.

FRAGRANT STIR-FRIED MORNING GLORY
TUMIS KANGKUNG

Morning glory, or water spinach as it is also known, grows in many parts of the world and is a beloved green that lends itself perfectly to the garlic, ginger and chilli flavours of Asian cuisine. In Indonesia, it can be found on restaurant menus everywhere, a stir-fried staple that is redolent with aromatics.

If you can't find morning glory, you can use other green vegetables such as spinach, kale, tenderstem broccoli, mangetout or green beans. To make this recipe vegetarian or vegan, you can replace the *terasi* or fish sauce with 1 tablespoon of light soy sauce mixed with 1 tablespoon of sesame oil.

Origin Popular all over Indonesia
Chilli heat Moderate
Sambal suggestion Caramelised shallot sambal bawang (p.200)
Serves 4 as a side

———

1 garlic clove, peeled and crushed
2cm piece of ginger (about 10g), peeled and grated
1 banana shallot or 2 Thai shallots, peeled and thinly sliced
2 long red chillies, deseeded and thinly sliced
300g morning glory (or similar Asian greens), chopped into long chunks
½ tsp terasi (or 2 tsp fish sauce)
Sea salt and white pepper, to taste
Coconut oil or sunflower oil, for frying

———

Heat 2 tablespoons of oil in a large frying pan over a medium heat. Fry the garlic, ginger, shallot and chillies until softened and aromatic, about 5–10 minutes. Add the morning glory with a splash of water, the terasi or fish sauce, and season with salt and pepper. Stir-fry for 2 minutes, making sure the stalks retain their bite. Serve immediately.

STIR-FRIED VEGETABLE CAP CAY
CAP CAY

This Chinese-Indonesian dish is a favourite in my family, and the one I crave when I want a veggie fix. *Cap cay* uses a medley of vegetables, often cauliflower, cabbage and carrot, but you can add any vegetables you have lying around. Adding cornflour helps thicken the sauce into a gravy that is delicious soaked up with rice. You can make it vegetarian by seasoning it with light soy sauce and sesame oil instead of oyster sauce, a little at a time.

Origin Popular all over Indonesia
Serves 4 as a side or 2 as a light main

1 head of cauliflower or broccoli, cut into bite-sized florets
2 carrots, peeled and thinly sliced on the diagonal
50g mangetout
3 small banana shallots or 6 Thai shallots, peeled and thinly sliced
4cm piece of ginger (about 20g), peeled and finely chopped
3 garlic cloves, peeled and thinly sliced
6 baby corn, halved lengthways
12 cherry tomatoes, halved
8 brown mushrooms, thinly sliced
240ml vegetable stock (p.248)
2 tbsp oyster sauce
1 tbsp cornflour mixed with 1 tbsp water
Sea salt and white pepper, to taste
Coconut oil or sunflower oil, for frying

To serve
1 spring onion, thinly sliced on the diagonal
Handful of Chinese celery leaves or coriander leaves

Bring a pan of salted water to the boil over a high heat. Blanch the cauliflower or broccoli florets for 1–2 minutes, until slightly undercooked. Drain and refresh under cold running water until cool, then set aside. Top up the boiling water, then repeat with the carrot slices and mangetout, blanching for 1½ minutes and 30 seconds respectively.

Heat 2 tablespoons of oil over a medium heat in a large wok or deep saucepan. Fry the shallots, ginger and garlic for 3–4 minutes until softened and fragrant. Add another 1 tablespoon of oil, then sauté the baby corn, tomatoes and mushrooms for 3 minutes. Add the remaining blanched vegetables and cook, stirring, for 1 minute. Pour in the stock and oyster sauce and bring to a simmer. Season with salt and white pepper.

Add 1 teaspoon of the cornflour mixture at a time until the sauce slightly thickens. Simmer for 2 minutes after the final addition of cornflour.

Remove from the heat and serve in a large serving dish. Garnish with the sliced spring onion and Chinese celery leaves or coriander leaves.

Variation: Chicken and prawn cap cay

Add 2 chicken breasts and 120g raw prawns to turn this dish into hearty main meal for two. Pan-fry bite-sized chicken pieces in 2 tablespoons of oil over a medium-high heat until just cooked through, then add the prawns and cook until they start to curl and become opaque and pink. Set aside. Prepare the recipe as above (using chicken stock, if you like) then add the cooked chicken and prawns to the pan along with the blanched vegetables to heat through.

VEGETABLE AND TEMPEH FRIED NOODLES
MIE GORENG SAYUR

Mie goreng, otherwise known as fried noodles, is so popular in Indonesia and around the world that there is even a *mie goreng* scented candle made in Australia. Also popular in Malaysia, Singapore and vast parts of South-East Asia, this stir-fried egg noodle dish is served at both ends of the Indonesian culinary spectrum, from high-end restaurants to roving street-food carts, tempting locals to dine on freshly made noodles as they pass through the neighbourhood.

My take on *mie goreng* is flavoured with cumin, coriander, garlic and ginger and a powerful umami-led combination of ketchup, light soy and kecap manis. Use rice noodles and omit the egg to make this recipe vegan. It will last up to 3 days in the fridge and is best served with *kerupuk* crackers for extra crunch.

Pictured overleaf

Origin Popular all over Indonesia
Sambal suggestion Caramelised shallot sambal bawang (p.200)
Serves 2

100g tempeh or fried, smoked or firm tofu, cut into 1 x 3cm chunks
225g baby potatoes, halved and cut into 2–3mm slices
240g fresh egg noodles or 100g dried egg noodles
1 tsp ground coriander
1 tsp ground cumin
3 tbsp tomato ketchup
2 tbsp kecap manis (p.254), plus optional extra for grilling
2 tbsp light soy sauce
Juice of ½ lime
½ head of broccoli, cut into bite-sized florets
4 shiitake mushrooms (or chestnut or brown mushrooms), stems removed, thinly sliced
2 small banana shallots or 4 Thai shallots, peeled and thinly sliced
2 garlic cloves, peeled and thinly sliced
4cm piece of ginger (about 20g), peeled and finely chopped
2 spring onions, thinly sliced on the diagonal
2 eggs, beaten
Sea salt and black pepper, to taste
Coconut oil or sunflower oil, for frying

To serve
Fried shallots (p.251), optional
Kerupuk (p.28) or prawn crackers

If using a wet tofu, spread the pieces in a single layer on top of several layers of paper towels and cover with additional paper towels. Let the tofu stand for 15 minutes, pressing down occasionally to squeeze out any excess moisture. This is not necessary for tempeh.

Heat 4 tablespoons of oil with a large pinch of salt in a frying pan over a high heat. When the oil is shimmering, add the tempeh or tofu and fry until golden, about 3–4 minutes. Drain on a tray lined with paper towels. Alternatively, if you prefer to grill your tempeh or tofu, brush it with a mixture of 1 tablespoon each of oil and kecap manis and place it under the grill on a high heat for 3–4 minutes each side.

Top up the pan with another 3–4 tablespoons oil, add a pinch of salt and return it to a high heat. When the oil is shimmering, fry the potato slices until golden all over and cooked through, about 6–8 minutes, adding more oil if necessary.

Continues overleaf

If using fresh egg noodles, poke a few holes in the packet and massage to separate them. If using dried egg noodles, cook them according to the packet instructions. Drain and set aside.

Mix the ground coriander, cumin, tomato ketchup, kecap manis, light soy sauce and lime juice in a small bowl and set aside.

Heat 2 tablespoons of oil in a large wok or frying pan over a high heat. When the oil is shimmering, add the broccoli and mushrooms and fry for 3 minutes until beginning to soften. Add another 1 tablespoon of oil, then add the shallots, garlic, ginger and spring onions and cook for a further 2 minutes. Push the ingredients to one side of the pan, add 1 teaspoon of oil, then pour in the beaten eggs. Allow the egg to set for 1 minute before stirring to scramble it, then stir it through the other ingredients.

Add the noodles to the pan, combining them with the other ingredients, then add the spice, soy and ketchup mixture. Continue cooking until the noodles are warmed through and the sauce has been absorbed by the ingredients. Season with salt and pepper, if needed.

Transfer to plates and serve immediately with a sprinkle of fried shallots and a side of crackers.

SWEET SOY TEMPEH
TEMPE MANIS

Tempe manis is a stir-fry that is rich, sweet and spicy all at once. The sweetness of the dish is a trademark of central Java, where I learnt the recipe – it's sticky with caramelised kecap manis and palm sugar, and perfectly balanced by the nutty flavour of crispy tempeh, the crunch of roasted peanuts and the gentle heat of the chilli. The scent of kaffir lime, lemongrass and ginger fills my kitchen every time I cook it, making it a favourite in our house that's quick and easy to prepare.

Best served with Red rice (p.246), *tempe manis* lasts for up to 3 days in the fridge.

──────

Origin Java
Chilli heat Moderate
Serves 4

──────

90g unsalted peanuts or unsalted roasted peanuts
400g tempeh, cut into 1 x 3cm chunks
Large pinch of salt
3 small banana shallots or 6 Thai shallots, peeled and thinly sliced
4 garlic cloves, peeled and thinly sliced
4 long red chillies, thinly sliced (deseeded if you prefer less heat)
1 lemongrass stalk, bruised and tied in a knot
4 kaffir lime leaves or 2 bay leaves
6 thin slices of ginger or galangal, skin on
200g mangetout, trimmed
3 tbsp kecap manis (p.254), plus optional extra for grilling
2 tbsp palm sugar or brown sugar mixed with 2 tbsp water
Sea salt, to taste
Coconut oil or sunflower oil, for frying

If roasting your own peanuts, preheat the oven to 200°C/180°C fan/gas 6, scatter the peanuts over a baking tray and bake for 5–10 minutes or until golden, shaking the tray during cooking so they roast evenly. Set aside. If using shop-bought roasted peanuts you can skip this step.

Heat 4 tablespoons of oil with a large pinch of salt in a frying pan over a high heat. When the oil is shimmering, add half the tempeh and fry until golden, about 3–4 minutes, then drain on a tray lined with paper towels. Repeat with the remaining tempeh, adding a little more oil if necessary. Alternatively, if you prefer to grill your tempeh, brush it with a mixture of 1 tablespoon each of oil and kecap manis and place it under the grill on a high heat for 3–4 minutes each side.

Heat 2 tablespoons of oil in a frying pan over a medium heat. Fry the shallots, garlic and chillies with the lemongrass, kaffir lime leaves and ginger or galangal until fragrant and softened. Increase the heat to high, add another 1 tablespoon of oil and cook the mangetout for 1 minute. Add the fried tempeh and roasted peanuts, stirring them continuously. Finally, add the kecap manis and sugar and water mix to the pan, stirring until it is caramelised and clinging to the ingredients. Season with salt. Remove the lemongrass stalk and slices of ginger or galangal, then serve immediately.

CRISPY SOY AND GINGER ROAST POTATOES
KENTANG KECAP DAN JAHE

These versatile potatoes are impossibly crispy, and it's a dish I love to serve as an impressive side alongside steaks at a summer barbecue or a Sunday roast. A stand-out accompaniment, the potatoes are roasted, then tossed with stir-fried spring onions and then drizzled with a rich soy dressing that is sharpened by the acidic hit of vinegar. In the same way that vinegar can make the crunchiest of chips go a little soggy, my soy and vinegar dressing has the same effect, so dress the potatoes only when you are ready to serve them.

———

Serves 4–6 as a side

———

1 large whole garlic bulb, halved widthways
1.2kg floury potatoes (such as Maris Piper), skin on and cut into 4cm chunks
Sea salt and black pepper, to taste
Sunflower oil, for roasting

For the stir-fried spring onions
8 spring onions, chopped into 3cm chunks
8 garlic cloves, peeled and thinly sliced
12cm ginger (about 60g), peeled and cut into long, thin matchsticks

For the soy dressing
4 tbsp rice vinegar or white wine vinegar
4 tbsp light soy sauce

Preheat the oven to 220°C/200°C fan/gas 7. Pour 6 tablespoons of oil into a very large roasting tray with the garlic bulb halves and a generous sprinkle of salt. Place the roasting tray in the oven to heat.

Put the potatoes into a large pan and cover with cold water. Add 1 tablespoon of salt and bring to the boil, then reduce the heat and simmer for 5 minutes. Drain the potatoes, then return them to the pan to steam for 2 minutes. As the potatoes are steaming, shake the pan to rough up their edges for maximum crispiness.

Remove the hot roasting tray from the oven and carefully add the potatoes in a single layer, being careful not to overcrowd the tray. Toss the potatoes in the hot oil until they are fully coated, then season generously with salt and pepper. Roast for 45 minutes or until golden and crispy, turning the potatoes over halfway to ensure even roasting.

In the last 10 minutes of the cooking time, prepare the stir-fried spring onions and the soy dressing. Heat 2 tablespoons of oil in a frying pan over a medium heat and add the spring onions, garlic and ginger. Cook for 2–3 minutes until fragrant and just beginning to soften, then remove from the heat. To make the dressing, mix the vinegar and soy sauce in a small bowl and set aside.

Once golden, toss the potatoes with the spring onion, garlic and ginger, then drizzle over the vinegar and soy dressing. Serve immediately.

SPICY BAKED AUBERGINE
TERUNG BALADO

This is a wonderful dish to make when you have people over for dinner, as it is substantial, incredibly easy to cook, can be reheated if prepared ahead of time and is loved by vegans and meat eaters alike.

The flavour in this dish comes from the spicy *balado* sauce. For this recipe I have used my tomato sambal, which gives a lovely mix of umami, sweetness and heat. Be generous with the sauce, as this is a dish that soaks up flavour. I like to serve it with finely chopped spring onion and fried shallots for crunch. It can be served as a main course with Coconut rice (p.246) and extra vegetables or with many other dishes as part of a much bigger feast.

Origin Popular all over Indonesia
Chilli heat Moderate
Serves 4

———

4 large aubergines
1 quantity of Tomato sambal (p.194)
1 spring onion, thinly sliced on the diagonal
1 tbsp Fried shallots (p.251)
Sea salt and black pepper, to taste
Coconut oil or sunflower oil, for roasting

———

Preheat the oven to 220ºC/200ºC fan/gas 7. Slice each aubergine in half lengthways. Score each flesh side diagonally in one direction, inserting the knife 1cm into the flesh, and then repeat in the opposite direction to create a crisscross pattern. Coat the scored flesh of each aubergine in oil and then, using a pastry brush or teaspoon, dab a small amount of the sambal on each aubergine. Season with salt and black pepper.

Place the aubergines on an oiled baking tray. Bake on the top shelf of the hot oven for 15 minutes. Remove from the oven and brush the aubergines with a little more oil. Return to the oven and bake for a further 10–15 minutes until the flesh is softened and cooked through.

To serve, coat the flesh of the aubergines with more sambal, then top with the spring onion and fried shallots. Serve any remaining sambal alongside for people to help themselves.

FISH & SEAFOOD

—

Eating seafood in Indonesia can be a spectacular affair, often set against the backdrop of shimmering white sand at twilight and accompanied by the mesmerising crashing of waves. As the sun sets on the Indonesian coast, a large golden disc disappearing into the horizon, the eateries that dot the shoreline are typically awash with diners tucking into platters laden with the freshest offerings of the sea. Fish such as snapper, grouper or mahi mahi and seafood such as prawns, squid and lobsters are grilled in wire baskets and turned over charcoal embers, then basted with boldly flavoured spice pastes, butter and kecap manis. These smoky, succulent delights are typically served with sambal, a refreshing side of cucumber, lettuce and tomato, and a healthy serving of rice.

Fish is always caught fresh that morning and then gutted and cleaned before being sent to the restaurant's door. At the *pasar ikan* (fish market) my open-toe sandals were a poor choice of footwear on the slippery tiles and cement floors, stained by fish blood and guts, that span several large hallways. These markets are everywhere along the coasts of Indonesia, an aquatic economy in the world's largest maritime country, with over 17,000 islands in its charge.

Fish and seafood are abundant here, far more affordable and easier to source than red meat, and so are prepared and served in endless ways. Across Indonesia you will find variations of fish satay (p.120), minced fish that is combined with spices and wrapped around lemongrass stems, then grilled over smoke and fire, a healthy and light meal that is as beautiful as it is satisfying.

In the Maluku islands where fishing villages thrive along the shorelines, tuna is chopped into small cubes and cured in a citrus, chilli, shallot and lemon basil dressing, in Indonesia's answer to ceviche (p.118).

For a fresh and simple dinner, fillets of fish can be pan-fried and served with most of the accompaniments you will find in the Sambal chapter. Crispy-skinned sea bass goes perfectly with the Fresh tomato and basil dabu-dabu (p.196) – a light and summery seafood lunch. Whole baked fish can be rubbed inside and out with an umami-rich Tomato sambal (p.194) or the Fresh Balinese sambal matah (p.206), which is fragrant with shallots, garlic, lemongrass and chilli and provides a freshness and zing that make for a perfect meal. Prawn satay is served with the fiery Sulawesi rica-rica chilli sauce (p.209), ideal for cooking on the griddle or barbecue. If you want to be transported to Bali, barbecue or griddle turmeric- and ginger-marinated squid and finish it with a butter and kecap manis glaze (p.124). It's a dish that will make you feel as though you're under the warm sun on even the coldest of days.

Always invest in the best-quality, freshest seafood you can afford and have your fishmonger clean and gut the fish for you – it makes life a whole lot easier. I am a strong believer in sourcing sustainable fish; the easiest way to do this is to look out for the blue label that means the fish is approved by the Marine Stewardship Council (MSC), which monitors fish stocks to combat overfishing. Mix and match spice pastes, sauces and glazes with different seafood and have fun with it. You can poach, steam, grill or fry it, but my favourite way is to barbecue seafood, giving it all the smoke and flavour of those shoreline grills on the Indonesian coast. A showstopping feast to be shared.

SPICE ISLANDS CEVICHE
GOHU IKAN TERNATE

This lime, chilli and basil ceviche hails from the Maluku Islands, an area nicknamed the Spice Islands in the sixteenth century by European traders due to the nutmeg, mace and cloves they found there. Surrounded by turquoise water, coral reefs, volcanoes and palm-tree-lined beaches, these islands are a paradise where fish is naturally the primary source of protein for locals. Unlike most Indonesians, who prefer to cook their meat or fish to the point of well done, the residents and many fishermen of the town of Ternate prepare fish raw or cure it ceviche-style, marinated in a citrus dressing with lemon basil. This recipe uses the traditional method of curing raw fish using the acid in citrus juice, so do try to buy the best-quality sashimi-grade fish you can find. I love this dish for its zingy freshness. It has just the right amount of heat with a perfectly balanced dressing that is sour and spicy, yet delicate.

Origin Ternate, Maluku Islands
Chilli heat Moderate
Serves 4 as a starter

——

300g skinless, boneless fillets of sashimi-grade fish, such as tuna, salmon, sea bass, snapper or sea bream
A drizzle of sunflower oil
Small handful of unsalted roasted peanuts, roughly chopped

For the marinade
2 long red chillies, thinly sliced (deseeded if you prefer less heat)
1 small banana shallot or 2 Thai shallots, peeled and finely chopped
Handful of lemon basil, Thai basil or Italian basil leaves, very thinly sliced, plus extra to garnish
Zest and juice of 5–6 limes, to taste
2–3 tsp palm sugar or brown sugar, to taste
Sea salt, to taste

——

To make the marinade, combine all the ingredients in a small bowl and set aside.

Slice the fish evenly into 1cm cubes and place in a large glass or other non-reactive bowl. (If you use a metal bowl, the ceviche may take on a metallic taste.) Pour the marinade over the fish and toss well to ensure all the pieces are fully coated. Leave to cure for 5 minutes. Season with salt.

Arrange the ceviche on a plate and drizzle with sunflower oil. Garnish with the chopped roasted peanuts and extra shredded basil leaves.

FISH AND PRAWN LEMONGRASS SATAY
SATE IKAN

There is much joy to be had from a freshly cooked fish and prawn satay. Found all over Indonesia at nearly every seaside town, it is most famous in Bali, where satay is presented as a food offering to the gods during Hindu ceremonies. Street-food vendors can be seen fanning the embers below skewers that line up like piano keys over their grills, minced, spiced and wrapped around a fragrant stem of lemongrass. Their small size makes them a great on-the-go snack.

My version uses soy, coriander and white pepper to enhance the flavour of the fish and prawns, with the subtle citrus of the lemongrass in every bite. For a main course, serve with a light salad or fried rice, a sambal and *kerupuk* or prawn crackers.

Origin Bali
Chilli heat Moderate (if served with sambal)
Makes 8 skewers

250g skinless, boneless white fish fillets, such
   as cod or sea bass
100g raw king prawns, peeled and deveined
2 egg yolks
½ bunch of coriander, finely chopped
50g trimmed green beans, thinly sliced
2 tsp light soy sauce
¼ tsp ground white pepper
¼ tsp sea salt
1–2 tbsp cornflour (optional)
Coconut oil or sunflower oil, for frying and grilling
Juice of 1 lime, plus extra lime wedges, to serve
1 quantity of Padang green chilli sambal (p.202),
   to serve (optional)

For the skewers
4 long, thick lemongrass stalks, cut in half
   lengthways, or 8 thick bamboo skewers

If using bamboo skewers, soak them in cold water for at least 30 minutes before preparing the satay. There is no need to soak lemongrass stalks.

Using paper towels, pat the fish and prawns dry and then roughly chop them into chunks. Place in a food processor along with the egg yolks and pulse briefly to a coarse paste. Try not to over-blend it, as you want it to retain some texture. Transfer the fish and prawn mixture to a large bowl and add the coriander, green beans, soy sauce, white pepper and salt. Stir together until mixed well.

To check the seasoning of the mixture, heat 1 teaspoon of oil in a frying pan over a medium-high heat. Take 1 teaspoon of the mixture and roll it into a flat patty, then fry on both sides until golden and cooked through (about 2–3 minutes). Taste it and adjust the seasoning as necessary. If the mixture feels a bit too loose to wrap around the skewers, add a little cornflour so that the mixture clings better to the skewers.

Oil your hands and mould the fish and prawn mixture around each lemongrass stalk or bamboo skewer, forming the cigar shape of a kofta. Chill the skewers in the fridge until ready to cook.

Place a large non-stick frying pan or griddle over a high heat. Add 1 tablespoon of oil to the pan (or brush the griddle with oil) and cook the skewers for about 5–6 minutes, turning every minute or so until they are cooked evenly and are golden all over. (They also cook beautifully on the barbecue – simply brush the skewers with oil before cooking over a medium-high heat and continue brushing with oil as you turn them.)

When cooked, squeeze plenty of fresh lime juice over the skewers and serve immediately with extra lime wedges and sambal to dip, if using.

CHILLI PRAWN SATAY WITH RICA-RICA
SATE UDANG RICA-RICA

This satay recipe is an easy and satisfying dish for those who like it hot. The *rica-rica* sambal from Sulawesi literally translates to 'chilli-chilli' – the repetition of the word a warning (or, depending on your preference, a celebration) of the hot chilli flavours enjoyed by the Manadonese people of Sulawesi.

Grilling the prawns on a barbecue gives extra char and flavour, but the result is just as juicy and delectable when cooked in a large frying pan or griddle according to the instructions opposite. Serve with *kerupuk* or prawn crackers, a fresh salad and fried rice.

——

Origin Manado, Sulawesi
Chilli heat Hot
Serves 4 as a starter

——

24 raw king prawns, body peeled and deveined, but heads and tails left intact
Juice of 1 lime
Sunflower oil, for frying

For the spice mix
¼ tsp chilli powder
¼ tsp ground coriander
¼ tsp ground cumin
¼ tsp ground black pepper
¼ tsp sea salt

To serve
1 quantity of Sulawesi rica-rica chilli sauce (p.209)
Kerupuk (p.28) or prawn crackers

For the skewers
4 long, thick lemongrass stalks, cut in half lengthways, or 8 thick bamboo or metal skewers

If using bamboo skewers, soak them in cold water for at least 30 minutes before preparing the satay. There is no need to soak lemongrass stalks.

To make the spice mix, combine all the ingredients in a small bowl.

To prepare the prawns, rub the lime juice and a little oil into them, then sprinkle the spice mix all over. Thread 3 prawns onto each skewer, then set aside.

Heat a large frying pan or griddle over a high heat. Add 1 tablespoon of oil to the pan (or brush the griddle with oil) and cook the satay skewers for 2 minutes each side, or until the prawns turn opaque with pink accents, have curled slightly and are just cooked through. (They also cook beautifully on the barbecue – simply brush the skewers with oil before cooking over a medium-high heat and continue to brush with oil as you turn them.)

Serve with the rica-rica chilli sauce to dip, and crackers alongside, if you like.

KECAP MANIS CALAMARI
CUMI BAKAR

This dish is inspired by the chefs on Jimbaran beach in Bali, who set up their grills on the sand and baste fish, squid and other seafood with a mixture of butter and kecap manis. It is so simple to prepare and the squid can easily be substituted with cuttlefish or prawns. The glaze also works on fish; generously spoon it over just before serving. Grilled calamari is best cooked quickly over a high, searing heat, which produces tender bites of sweet, salty, buttery squid that transport your taste buds to the shorelines of Bali. Serve with a tomato and cucumber salad, Red rice (p.246) and *sambal matah*, just as they do on Jimbaran, if you like.

Origin Bali
Sambal suggestion Fresh Balinese sambal matah (p.206)
Serves 4 as a starter

500g whole squid, cleaned
3 garlic cloves, peeled and crushed
3cm piece of ginger (about 15g), peeled and grated
¼ tsp ground turmeric
Juice of 1 lime
Pinch of sea salt
1 tbsp sunflower oil

For the glaze
30g unsalted butter, melted
2 tbsp kecap manis (p.254)
2 tbsp sunflower oil

To serve
Juice of 1 lime, plus extra lime wedges
Kecap manis (p.254)
Small handful of lemon basil, Thai basil or Italian basil leaves

Slice the squid into 5mm rings and chop each tentacle into chunks. In a large bowl, mix together the garlic, ginger, turmeric, lime juice, salt and oil. Add the squid, stir to coat, then leave to marinate for 15 minutes in the fridge.

Stir the glaze ingredients together in a bowl. Oil a barbecue, griddle or frying pan and cook the squid rings in batches, if needed, brushing each ring with the glaze as it cooks. Cook the squid rings for about 1–2 minutes on each side, or until they start to curl and are just tender.

Arrange the calamari on a large serving platter. Squeeze over the lime juice, drizzle with kecap manis, scatter over the basil leaves and serve with extra wedges of lime and more kecap manis on the side.

OVEN-BAKED FISH WITH SAMBAL
IKAN BAKAR

Ikan bakar comes in many forms all over Indonesia, but the basic principle is to season the fish with lime juice and a spiced marinade, then wrap it in banana leaves and cook it over charcoal. In this version the fish is baked in the oven on top of slices of lime until the flesh is opaque and flaking, but it can also be wrapped in a foil parcel or banana leaf and grilled on a barbecue.

I've suggested using *sambal matah* or tomato sambal as the marinade here, but you can use any chilli-based sambal and the result will be utterly delicious. If you prefer, you can use two smaller fish weighing 400–600g each instead of one whole large fish and just reduce the cooking time to 15–20 minutes. Serve with vegetables, Crispy soy and ginger roast potatoes (p.108) and extra sambal, if you like.

Origin Popular all over Indonesia
Chilli heat Moderate
Serves 4

1.5kg whole sea bream or similar firm-fleshed white fish, cleaned and gutted
3 quantities of Fresh Balinese sambal matah (p.206) or Tomato sambal (p.194)
2 lemongrass stalks, bruised and tied in a knot
3 limes, plus extra wedges to serve
Sea salt, to taste
Sunflower oil, for drizzling and brushing

Remove the fish from the fridge about 15 minutes before cooking to let it come up to room temperature. Preheat the oven to 220ºC/200ºC fan/gas 7.

Divide the sambal into two bowls: put two thirds in one bowl for coating the fish and keep the remaining third to serve.

Using a sharp knife, score the fish 3 or 4 times on the diagonal on both sides. Drizzle lightly with oil and season with the juice of 1 lime and a pinch of salt. Put the lemongrass inside the cavity of the fish, along with most of the sambal set aside for coating the fish. (If using a cooked sambal, ensure it has cooled before spooning it into the fish.) Spread the remaining sambal for coating over the fish skin and into the scored cuts.

Lay a large sheet of foil on a baking tray and brush it with oil. Thinly slice the remaining 2 limes and arrange the slices across the foil, then lay the fish on top. Bake in the hot oven for 30–35 minutes. (This dish also cooks beautifully on the barbecue. Simply wrap the fish in oiled sheets of foil or in a prepared banana leaf, p.253, held together with cocktail sticks, then place the fish parcel over a medium-high heat and cook for 25–35 minutes.) To check if the fish is cooked, insert a thin-bladed knife into the flesh, leave it there for 30 seconds and then remove – if the blade is piping hot, the fish is cooked through. If it is not quite ready, return the fish to the oven and test again every 5 minutes.

Serve the fish with the remaining sambal and extra wedges of lime.

CRISPY FISH WITH SAMBAL BAWANG
IKAN GORENG

One of my father's favourite dishes is *ikan gurami goreng*, a dish found all over Indonesia consisting of deep-fried freshwater fish served with a sambal. I've chosen a rich caramelised shallot, chilli and garlic sambal here as it complements the fish beautifully. In some restaurants, they butterfly the fish in such a way that each fillet is peeled off the skeleton and fried with such precision that the fillets are suspended in the air, giving the impression that the fish is flying off the plate with wings on either side. This crunchy edible fish statue is my idea of heaven.

To recreate this recipe, I've opted for battered fish fillets, which are far easier to fry in a humble domestic kitchen than a whole fish. The batter is spiced with chilli, pepper and the earthy notes of coriander, and the caramelised sambal is drizzled over the crunchy batter just before serving. Frying times will vary depending on the thickness and weight of the fish: 125–140g fillets will take 3–5 minutes, while 140–180g fillets will take 5–7 minutes. This dish is best served with Turmeric yellow rice (p.247) and a side of green vegetables.

Origin Popular all over Indonesia
Chilli heat Hot
Serves 4

---

4 skinless, boneless thick white fish fillets, such as cod (about 500–700g in total)
1 quantity of Caramelised shallot sambal bawang (p.200), to serve
Lime wedges, to serve (optional)
Sea salt and white pepper, to taste
Sunflower oil, for deep-frying

For the batter
110g cornflour
1 tsp ground chilli powder
2 tsp ground coriander
2 tsp sea salt
2 tsp ground white pepper
4 medium eggs

To make the batter, sift the cornflour into a mixing bowl with the ground spices, salt and pepper. Gradually whisk in the eggs, adding them one at a time, until the batter is smooth and free of any lumps. (A few minutes of vigorous whisking should do the trick, but if it needs extra help pass the batter through a sieve after whisking to remove any remaining lumps.)

Pat the fish fillets dry with a paper towel and season lightly with salt and pepper. Fill a large, deep-sided saucepan one-third full with oil and heat the oil to 180°C. (If you do not have a kitchen thermometer, check the oil is at temperature by adding a cube of bread; it should turn golden in 15 seconds.)

Dip the fish fillets into the batter and carefully lower them into the hot oil. You may need to do this in batches. Depending on the size of your fillets, fry the fish for 3–7 minutes or until the batter is golden. To check if the fish is cooked, insert a thin-bladed knife into the flesh of the fish, leave it there for 30 seconds and then remove — if the blade is piping hot, the fish is cooked through.

To serve, place the fish on a serving platter and spoon a generous helping of the sambal on top of each fillet. Serve with extra sambal on the side and wedges of lime, if you like.

PAN-FRIED DABU-DABU SEA BASS
IKAN GORENG DABU-DABU

This recipe is adapted from a glorious dish I tasted in Northern Sulawesi. There, the locals often fry their fish whole and top it with the *dabu-dabu Manado* sambal of tomatoes, lemon basil, chilli and lime juice that is typical of the region. My version uses sea bass fillets that are seasoned with lime juice, pan-fried to crispy-skin perfection, then served with the fragrance of the *dabu-dabu* relish alongside. Add a helping of Crispy soy and ginger roast potatoes (p.108) to make it a heartier offering.

Origin Manado, Sulawesi
Chilli heat Moderate
Serves 4

——

Juice of 1 lime
4 skin-on, boneless sea bass fillets or other boneless white fish fillets (about 140g each)
A knob of unsalted butter
Sea salt and black pepper, to taste
Coconut oil or sunflower oil, for frying

To serve
Lime wedges
Small handful of lemon basil, Thai basil or Italian basil leaves
1 quantity of Fresh tomato and basil dabu-dabu (p.196)

——

Squeeze the lime juice onto the flesh side of the fish fillets, then season all over with a little salt and pepper.

Heat 2 tablespoons of oil in a frying pan over a high heat. When the oil is shimmering, turn the heat down to medium and lay the fish fillets in the pan, skin-side down. (You may need to do this in two batches, depending on the size of your pan.) Press each fillet down with a fish slice to prevent it from curling. Leave the fish to cook for 3–4 minutes undisturbed, until you can see it is cooked three quarters of the way up the flesh and the skin underneath is crispy and golden.

Add the knob of butter to the pan and, as it begins to melt, flip the fillets over and fry for 30 seconds or until they are just cooked through.

Serve immediately with wedges of lime, torn basil leaves and the dabu-dabu relish on the side.

PRAWN COCONUT CURRY
GULAI UDANG

This spiced coconut milk curry is a healthy, delicious dish that is quick to prepare and ideal for a weeknight meal. With *gulai udang* you can vary the heat of the curry by adjusting the colour and strength of the chillies. If you feel like a milder, mellower curry, use red chillies. If you prefer the taste of sharper and more bitter green chillies, use green tomatoes and add an extra pinch of sugar for balance. Warming and gently spiced, this delicious prawn curry is best served with *kerupuk* or prawn crackers, rice and a little extra sambal on the side.

Origin Popular all over Indonesia
Chilli heat Moderate
Sambal suggestion Padang green chilli sambal (p.202)
Serves 4

2 tbsp coconut oil or sunflower oil
3 red or green tomatoes (ideally matching the colour of the chillies), chopped
1 tbsp ground coriander
400ml coconut milk
Large pinch of sea salt
Large pinch of ground white pepper
3 tsp palm sugar or brown sugar
3 tbsp fish sauce, or to taste
Juice of 1–2 limes, to taste, plus lime wedges to serve
400g raw king prawns, peeled and deveined but with tails left intact
130g baby corn, halved lengthways
75g mangetout
Chinese celery leaves or coriander leaves, chopped, to garnish
Kerupuk (p.28) or prawn crackers, to serve

For the spice paste
6 long red or green chillies, sliced (deseeded if you prefer less heat)
6 small banana shallots or 12 Thai shallots, peeled and sliced
6 garlic cloves, peeled and sliced
9cm piece of ginger (about 45g), peeled and sliced
Handful of candlenuts, macadamias, almonds or cashews, toasted for best flavour
2 lemongrass stalks, woody layers removed, thinly sliced
2 kaffir lime leaves, stems removed, very thinly sliced, or the zest of 1 lime

Place all the spice paste ingredients in a food processor and blend until smooth. Heat the oil in a large, deep saucepan over a medium heat and add the spice paste. Stirring continuously, cook the spice paste for 10–15 minutes or until fragrant and softened.

Add the chopped tomatoes and ground coriander to the pan and cook, stirring, for 1 minute. Pour the coconut milk and 200ml water into the pan and bring to the boil, then lower the heat and simmer for 30 minutes until thickened, stirring occasionally. Season to taste with the salt, pepper, sugar, fish sauce and lime juice. Reduce the sauce a little more, until thickened.

Add the prawns, baby corn and mangetout to the curry, stirring for 3–4 minutes until the prawns turn opaque with pink accents, have curled slightly and are just cooked through.

Divide the curry between four serving bowls and garnish with a sprinkling of chopped herbs. Serve with crackers and wedges of lime to squeeze over.

PRAWN AND CHICKEN FRIED NOODLES
MIE GORENG UDANG

Mie goreng translates as 'fried noodles' and there are as many variations as there are islands in Indonesia. Common to each version are the chewy egg noodles that form the base of the dish, coated in a delicious sweet and salty sauce, stirred together with vegetables, meat, tofu or seafood.

Enjoyed by both young and old alike, this comforting Indonesian meal will satisfy even the fussiest of little eaters and is a great meal to cook for the whole family. It's a dish that can be made from whatever is lurking in your fridge or pantry, so feel free to swap out the prawns and chicken for tofu and include any greens that need using up. Serve with *kerupuk* or prawn crackers for extra crunch.

Origin Popular all over Indonesia
Sambal suggestion Fermented shrimp sambal terasi (p.208)
Serves 4

480g fresh egg noodles or 200g dried egg noodles
4 skinless, boneless chicken thighs (about 330g total weight), cut into bite-sized pieces
3 garlic cloves, peeled and thinly sliced
2 eggs, beaten
225g raw king prawns, peeled and deveined
200g mangetout
3 tbsp light soy sauce
2 tbsp kecap manis (p.254)
2 tbsp fish sauce
2 tbsp tomato ketchup
½ tsp ground white pepper
1 tsp ground cumin
1 tsp ground coriander
Coconut oil or sunflower oil, for frying

To serve
2 spring onions, thinly sliced on the diagonal
Kerupuk (p.28) or prawn crackers

If using fresh egg noodles, poke a few holes in the packet and massage to separate them. If using dried egg noodles, cook according to the packet instructions. Drain and set aside.

Heat 3 tablespoons of oil in a deep, heavy-based saucepan over a high heat. When the oil is shimmering, add the chicken pieces. Fry the chicken until it begins to brown and you can no longer see any raw pinkness, then add the sliced garlic and fry for 1 minute, stirring continuously. Push the chicken to one side of the pan and add another 2 teaspoons of oil. Pour the beaten eggs into the oil and allow the eggs to set for 1 minute before stirring briefly to scramble them, then stir everything together. Add the prawns and mangetout and cook for another 2 minutes, adding a little more oil if the pan looks dry. Stir continuously so it does not burn.

Add the noodles to the pan and stir well to combine with the rest of the ingredients. Finally, add the soy, kecap manis, fish sauce, tomato ketchup and the spices to the pan and stir well to warm everything through.

Divide the noodles between four serving plates and serve immediately with a sprinkle of spring onions and a side of crackers.

POULTRY
& EGGS

—

Walking down the streets of Yogyakarta in central Java, you would be hard pressed not to find a chicken satay vendor fanning smoke from a small, mobile charcoal grill that sits on the pavement. These vendors, often women, sit by the road in traditional batik-patterned dress in front of an array of chicken skewers, banana leaf, compressed rice and peanut sauce. A popular street food for both passing tourists and locals, chicken satay can be purchased for little more than the spare change in your pocket.

When I think of satay it brings back memories of my father, wearing flip flops and the shortest of 1980s shorts in our Australian backyard, standing over the barbecue with enormous tongs and billowing smoke rising into the air. His chicken satay (p.140) was marinated in a simple kecap manis and lime dressing, served on the outdoor table with peanut sauce and my grandmother's pickle. The edges of the satay would crisp up and char, with a smokiness that only a coal fire provides – while the insides were juicy and cooked to perfection. Dad always joked that he was useless in the kitchen, but if you gave him a barbecue, he'd never let us down.

Indonesia is a country that knows how to cook chicken. Prepared in a variety of ways, you'll find chicken poached tenderly in aromatic broths (p.68), cooked and shredded for chicken rice porridge (p.71), wrapped in banana leaves and slow-cooked over burning coconut husks (p.150) and stir-fried with native leaves and spices (p.146). One of the most popular dishes of all is fried chicken, which can be found on almost every street corner. A common style involves frying the chicken in a spiced batter, and then smashing it with a granite *ulekan* (pestle) and coating it in a fiery chilli sambal, a dish known as *ayam penyet* (p.142). My own love affair with Indonesian chicken began at an early age. I remember the steaming platters of my grandmother Popo's Balinese spiced chicken marinated in a garlic, shallot, chilli and turmeric spice paste (p.150) that caramelised as it roasted in the oven, presented on the dinner table alongside big mountains of rice and vegetables.

Outside of the cities, you will see muscular free-range fowl roaming the dusty streets of the countryside among the rice crops and makeshift housing. They are *ayam kampung* (village chicken) and are bred in high enough numbers to feed families small quantities of eggs and a variety of chicken dishes that form a major part of the cuisine. These chickens get plenty of exercise, so are a little tougher, leaner and stringier to eat than their commercially bred cousins.

I often marvel at the many uses of eggs in Indonesian cuisine. Duck eggs are prized for their rich and creamy yolks, and are often served halved and hard-boiled, whisked and scrambled together with fried rice, or fried sunny side up and laid upon noodles and rice as the ultimate party hat. Chicken eggs are more common, especially in the villages where *ayam kampung* dominate. My aunty Tje Ie loves to fry her boiled eggs, giving them a crispy, browned and slightly wrinkled skin. She then stir-fries the eggs with a punchy chilli and coriander seed sauce to create *telur bumbu merah* (fried spiced soft-boiled eggs, p.158), one of my mother's favourites. Eggs are also used as a fantastic substitute when meat is scarce – such as in my beef rendang, which can be made with tofu and hard-boiled eggs (p.168).

There is a vibrance and variety in the poultry and egg dishes that Indonesians love to eat every day. There are slow-cooked recipes like the green chilli duck legs I encountered in West Sumatra, with the meat falling off the bone and coated in caramelised duck fat and spices (p.154). For those who love a quick stir-fry that packs a punch, there's *manu paokula*, a succulent flash-fried chicken dish with artichokes and kale that hails from the small island of Sumba (p.146), and Acehnese chicken, which is fragrant with fresh curry leaves reminiscent of the Indian-influenced cuisine of the region (p.152). Whatever cooking process is used, poultry and egg dishes offer a true insight into the archipelago – food that is textured, comforting, boldly spiced and mouthwateringly delicious.

CHICKEN SATAY WITH PEANUT SAUCE
SATE AYAM MADURA

Sweet, sour and salty marinated chicken thighs served with creamy spiced peanut sauce and tangy cucumber pickle is a recipe my grandmother and father have cooked for as long as I can remember. A barbecue gives the satay skewers an unbeatable smoky char, but a griddle or large frying pan will also do the trick.

This crowd-pleaser is a dish I often cook when entertaining, and it's loved by adults and kids alike. It's good with a side of Asian greens, Brown rice (p.245) and *kerupuk* crackers.

___

Origin Madura Island, Northeast Java
Chilli heat Mild
Serves 2 as a main or 4 as a starter

___

400g skinless, boneless chicken thighs, cut into 2cm dice
2 tbsp coconut oil or sunflower oil
1 quantity of Peanut sauce (p.204)
1 quantity of Cucumber, chilli and shallot pickle (p.88), to serve
Kerupuk (p.28) or prawn crackers, to serve

For the marinade
Zest of 1 lime
3 tbsp kecap manis (p.254)
¼ tsp salt
¼ tsp ground black pepper

For the glaze
3 tbsp kecap manis (p.254)
Juice of ½ lime

You will need 8–12 bamboo skewers, soaked in water for at least 30 minutes before use so they do not burn during cooking.

To make the marinade, combine the ingredients in a large bowl. Add the chicken, toss to coat the pieces evenly and leave to marinate in the fridge for at least 15 minutes, but preferably for 1 hour.

Place the ingredients for the glaze in a small saucepan over a high heat and reduce until thickened. Set aside.

Remove the marinated chicken from the fridge 15 minutes before cooking to let it come to room temperature. Thread 4–5 chicken pieces onto each of the soaked skewers.

When ready to cook, heat a large griddle or frying pan over a high heat. (You can also cook these skewers on a barbecue, if you like.) Brush the griddle with some of the oil or add the oil to the frying pan and, once hot, add the chicken skewers – you should hear a good sizzle! Cook the chicken for 6–8 minutes or until cooked through, rotating the skewers every couple of minutes. While it cooks, brush it with the prepared glaze. Once cooked, rest for 5 minutes.

To serve, pour a generous puddle of peanut sauce on the middle of the plate. Arrange the skewers on top of the peanut sauce. Drain the pickles from the liquid and serve on the side, along with crackers.

___

Variation: Tofu satay

To make this recipe vegan, substitute the chicken with a very firm tofu cut into 2cm dice. Marinate the tofu overnight, and cook the tofu skewers under a hot grill. Baste the tofu continually with the glaze until warmed through.

SMASHED FRIED CHICKEN WITH SAMBAL
AYAM PENYET

Ayam penyet is a dish that hails from Surabaya in East Java, where the chicken is marinated, boiled, fried and then smashed using an *ulekan* (pestle) before being smothered with a fiery sambal. When I first made this dish at home, initially I was reluctant to smash the crispy batter on my fried chicken pieces – it looked so perfect. But once I got started, I understood the satisfaction in doing so. The shards of crispy batter shatter and combine with juicy shreds of moist chicken, all mixed together with a layer of sambal running through it. It is absolute textural heaven.

I have adapted the traditional recipe, as I find that brining the chicken first gives it a juicy, full-flavoured succulence. Together with the spice rub, buttermilk and sambal, it makes for a finger-licking dish that deserves to be eaten with your hands. I've offered two types of sambal to accompany this dish; if you love spicy food, opt for the hotter Sulawesi *rica-rica* chilli sauce, but if you're in the mood for something milder, try it with my tomato sambal.

It's best served straight from the fryer while still hot, but it will last for up to 2 days in the fridge. You can reheat the chicken in the oven at 170°C/150°C fan/gas 3 for 10 minutes. Serve with Turmeric pickle (p.89), Crispy soy and ginger roast potatoes (p.108) and greens.

Pictured overleaf

Origin Surabaya, East Java
Chilli heat Moderate to hot
Serves 4

———

8–12 skin-on, bone-in chicken thighs
   and drumsticks
1¾ tbsp sea salt
200g plain flour
1½ tbsp cornflour
250ml buttermilk (or 235ml whole milk mixed with
   1 tbsp rice vinegar or white wine vinegar)
2 egg whites
2 tbsp vodka or other neutral clear spirit
Sunflower oil, for deep-frying
1 quantity of Tomato sambal (p.194) or Sulawesi
   rica-rica chilli sauce (p.209), to serve

For the spice mix
1½ tbsp sea salt
1½ tbsp ground coriander
1½ tbsp ground cumin
¾ tsp ground turmeric
¾ tsp ground nutmeg
1½ tbsp ground white pepper
1½ tsp ground black pepper

Place the chicken pieces on a tray and, 30 minutes before you are ready to cook, sprinkle 1 tablespoon of the salt all over the meat. Leave at room temperature for 30 minutes. You must then fry the chicken immediately, otherwise it will spoil.

Meanwhile, combine the ingredients for the spice mix. Place half of it in a mixing bowl and set aside. Place the other half in another mixing bowl and stir in the plain flour, the remaining ¾ tablespoon salt and the cornflour. In a third bowl, lightly whisk together the buttermilk, egg whites and vodka to make the batter.

When the chicken has nearly finished brining, fill a deep saucepan one-third full with oil and heat it to 160°C. (If you do not have a kitchen thermometer, check the oil is at temperature by adding a cube of bread; it should turn golden in 25–30 seconds.)

Once the chicken has brined in the salt for 30 minutes, you can coat it in the spices and flour. Without wiping the salt off (I find it gives added flavour), dip the chicken pieces first in the spice mix and then in the spiced flour, ensuring each piece is completely coated and shaking off any excess flour. Arrange the chicken pieces on a tray, ready to be battered and fried.

When you are ready to fry the chicken, dip the flour-coated pieces into the buttermilk batter and carefully lower them straight into the hot oil. Working in batches, fry the chicken pieces for about 10–12 minutes or until dark golden and crispy, depending on the size of the pieces. To test if they are cooked through, the thighs and drumsticks should be cooked to 82°C. (If you do not have a probe thermometer, make a small slice into the thickest part of the chicken – it is cooked when the juices run clear and the meat is fibrous inside, with no opaque pink flesh.) Once cooked, remove the fried chicken from the hot oil and place on a wire rack set over a baking tray lined with paper towels to allow any excess oil to drain – the chicken may lose its crispness if left to rest directly on paper towels.

The chicken will look crispy, golden and beautiful, but the tradition in Indonesia is to smash the batter on the chicken and then drizzle it with a delicious sambal. Place each chicken piece on a chopping board and bash it with a pestle, mallet or rolling pin using a little force. You only need to bash it on one side. Smear the sambal over the smashed chicken surface and serve immediately.

STIR-FRIED SUMBA CHICKEN
MANU PAOKULA

This dish from the island of Sumba is traditionally made with a steamed marinated chicken that is chopped and then stir-fried with banana blossom, cassava leaves and papaya leaves. The flavours have stayed with me, but the ingredients are a stretch to get outside of Indonesia, so I have created an adapted version that does it justice. Preserved marinated artichokes have the same texture and a similar flavour to the banana blossoms, while the cassava and papaya leaves are easily interchangeable with kale. If you can find smoked artichokes, you will get a taste of the smoky flavours of the traditional Sumba chicken, a beautiful contrast to the spice and flavour of the marinade.

Best eaten with rice and *sambal bawang, manu paokula* keeps for up to 3 days in the fridge.

Origin Sumba
Chilli heat Moderate
Sambal suggestion Caramelised shallot sambal bawang (p.200)
Serves 4

400g kale, woody stems removed, leaves thinly sliced
4 garlic cloves, peeled and finely chopped
3 small banana shallots or 6 Thai shallots, peeled and finely chopped
8 long red chillies, finely chopped (deseeded if you prefer less heat)
500g smoked artichokes or artichokes preserved in oil, drained and thinly sliced
Large handful of lemon basil, Thai basil or Italian basil leaves
Sea salt and white pepper, to taste
Coconut oil or sunflower oil, for frying

For the marinated chicken
4 garlic cloves, peeled
2 small banana shallots or 4 Thai shallots, peeled and roughly chopped
6 long red chillies, sliced (deseeded if you prefer less heat)
6 skinless, boneless chicken thighs, sliced into thin strips

To make the marinade, place the garlic, shallots and chillies together in a small food processor and blend to form a semi-coarse spice paste.

Heat 2 tablespoons of oil in a pan and cook the spice paste until fragrant and softened, about 10 minutes. Allow to cool, then mix the chicken strips with the spice paste, season with a pinch of salt and white pepper, and leave to marinate in the fridge for 30 minutes to 1 hour.

Meanwhile, blanch the kale in boiling salted water for 3 minutes, then refresh under cold running water until cool. Squeeze out any excess water from the kale and press between paper towels. Set aside.

Heat 3 tablespoons of oil in a wok or large frying pan, add the garlic, shallots and chillies and stir-fry until fragrant, about 10–15 minutes. Add the marinated chicken strips and stir-fry until no raw pinkness can be seen, about 3 minutes. Add the blanched kale, artichokes and a pinch of salt and pepper, adding a little more oil if the mixture looks dry. Stir-fry for a further 2 minutes, checking that the chicken is cooked through. Throw in the basil leaves for the final 30 seconds of cooking. Transfer to a large serving platter and serve immediately.

ROASTED CHILLI COCONUT CHICKEN
AYAM BUMBU RUJAK

The sauce for this dish is known as *rujak*. It imparts warmth to the chicken from its chilli heat, as well as fragrance from the garlic, creaminess from the coconut and a sour note from the tamarind. Traditionally, the chicken is chargrilled over hot coals, a trademark of this style of Indonesian cooking. In my version, a whole chicken sits in a bath of the delicious *rujak* sauce and is roasted in the oven at a searingly high heat. Serve with Crispy soy and ginger roast potatoes (p.108) and greens.

Pictured overleaf

Origin Java
Chilli heat Moderate
Serves 4

---

15 long red chillies (about 180g), roughly chopped
5 garlic cloves, peeled
2 kaffir lime leaves or 1 bay leaf
1.6kg whole chicken
1 lemongrass stalk, bruised and tied in a knot
4cm piece of ginger (about 20g), sliced
1 lime, halved, plus the juice of 1–2 limes
400ml coconut milk
400ml good-quality chicken stock (p.250)
1 tbsp palm sugar or brown sugar
2 tsp tamarind paste
Sea salt, to taste
Coconut oil or sunflower oil

Place the chillies and garlic in a small food processor together with 1½ tablespoons of oil and blend to a paste.

Heat 3 tablespoons of oil in a frying pan over a medium heat and fry the chilli paste with the kaffir lime leaves or bay leaf. Fry the paste until the oil separates, about 10 minutes. Allow to cool.

Spread one third of the paste under the skin of the chicken: starting at the neck, gently slide your fingers under the skin and work your way down, carefully separating the skin from the meat without tearing it. You can also work from the other side to reach the thighs. Rub the paste beneath the loosened skin, then massage the chicken from the outside to distribute the paste evenly. Stuff the cavity with the lemongrass, ginger and lime halves. Cover and leave to marinate in the fridge for 2 hours or more. If you don't have time to marinate, proceed straight to the next step.

Remove the chicken from the fridge 30 minutes before roasting to come to room temperature. Preheat the oven to 220ºC/200ºC fan/gas 7. Rub oil, salt and the juice of half a lime over the skin of the chicken. Combine the remaining paste with the coconut milk, stock, sugar, tamarind paste and a pinch of salt in a deep, large ovenproof tray, and place the whole chicken in the centre.

Roast for 15 minutes at 220ºC/200ºC fan/gas 7, then reduce the temperature to 200ºC/180ºC fan/gas 6 and roast for 1 hour or until the chicken is cooked through. The breast should be cooked to 75ºC and the thighs and legs to 82ºC. (If you do not have a probe thermometer, check by making a small slice into the thickest part of the chicken. It is cooked when the juices run clear and the meat is fibrous inside, with no opaque pink flesh.)

Once cooked, transfer the chicken to a board and cover with foil to keep it warm while it rests for 15 minutes. Meanwhile, transfer the sauce to a pan and reduce over a high heat for 10 minutes until it has thickened slightly. Adjust the seasoning with a little more lime juice and salt, if needed.

Serve the roast chicken on a large serving platter with the rujak sauce drizzled over and beneath it, with any leftover sauce served in a jug.

SPICED BALINESE ROAST CHICKEN
AYAM BETUTU

For this dish, traditionally a whole bird is rubbed with a Balinese spice paste, then wrapped in leaves before being buried in the earth or a claypot and covered with hot charcoals and burning coconut husks. When ready, the charred green parcel is opened to reveal steaming, tender chicken that is succulent and smoky with Balinese spices.

My version uses these traditional flavours but an easier technique, just like my grandmother Popo used to do. The rendered chicken fat with the kale and the spiced crispy skin makes it one of my favourite dishes. Serve with Red rice (p.246) and *sambal matah*.

———

Origin Bali
Chilli heat Moderate
Sambal suggestion Fresh Balinese sambal
  matah (p.206)
Serves 4

———

4 skin-on, bone-in chicken legs
400g kale, woody stems removed and leaves sliced
Sea salt and black pepper, to taste
Coconut oil or sunflower oil

For the spice paste
8cm piece of ginger (about 40g), peeled and sliced
6 garlic cloves, peeled and sliced
2 small banana shallots or 4 Thai shallots, peeled
  and sliced
3 long red chillies, sliced
¼ tsp ground turmeric
¼ tsp ground black pepper
¼ tsp ground white pepper
¼ tsp ground nutmeg
1 tsp ground coriander
¼ tsp sea salt
½ tbsp coconut oil or sunflower oil

Preheat the oven to 220°C/200°C fan/gas 7. Rub oil, salt and pepper onto the chicken legs. Heat 1 tablespoon of oil in a large frying pan over a medium heat and lay the chicken legs skin-side down in the pan (you may need to do this in batches, depending on the size of your pan). When the skin is crispy and golden, which will take about 12–15 minutes, turn the chicken over and cook it for a further 4 minutes on the other side. Reserve any of the rendered chicken fat for the kale.

Meanwhile, place the spice paste ingredients in a small food processor and blend to a semi-coarse paste. Heat 2 tablespoons of oil in a frying pan over a medium heat and fry the paste until fragrant, about 10–15 minutes. Set aside and allow to cool.

Blanch the kale in a pan of boiling salted water for 3 minutes, then run it under cold water to cool. Squeeze out any excess water and press it between paper towels. Mix a quarter of the spice paste with the kale, along with the chicken fat and a sprinkling of salt, then spread onto a baking tray.

Brush the remaining spice paste on the chicken; it should spread nicely over the skin. Place the chicken legs on a wire rack above the kale (if you don't have a wire rack the chicken can sit directly on the kale).

Bake on the top shelf for 30–35 minutes. If the spice paste starts to burn on the chicken skin, cover any blackened bits with foil and continue cooking. To check if the chicken is cooked, the legs should reach 82°C. (If you do not have a probe thermometer you can also check by making a small slice into the thickest part of the chicken. The chicken is cooked when the juices run clear and the meat is fibrous inside, with no opaque pink flesh.)

Once cooked, arrange the chicken legs and kale on individual plates and serve immediately.

ACEHNESE CHICKEN WITH CURRY LEAVES
AYAM TANGKAP ACEH

I first tried this dish on a beach in Sanur, Bali, and fell in love with the crispy fried curry leaves that adorned the plate. The dish itself hails from Aceh in North Sumatra, but it is famed all over the region. Traditionally it is served completely covered in the crispy curry leaves but, for ease of cooking at home, a single bunch gives just the right amount of balance. It's important to use fresh curry leaves for this recipe – the dried variety simply won't do the dish justice.

Serve with Brown rice (p.245) and a side of Padang green chilli sambal.

Origin Aceh, North Sumatra
Chilli heat Hot
Sambal suggestion Padang green chilli sambal (p.202)
Serves 4

---

1 tsp ground turmeric
Juice of 1 lime
800g skinless, boneless chicken thighs, cut into even, bite-sized chunks
Bunch of fresh curry leaves (about 30–40 leaves)
10 kaffir lime leaves, or the zest of 2 limes
1 lemongrass stalk, woody outer layers removed, thinly sliced
4 spring onions, cut into 2cm pieces
Sea salt and black pepper, to taste
Coconut oil or sunflower oil, for frying

For the spice paste
12cm piece of ginger (about 60g), peeled and sliced
8 small banana shallots or 16 Thai shallots, peeled and sliced
8 garlic cloves, peeled and sliced
4 long red chillies, sliced
4 long green chillies, sliced
2 lemongrass stalks, woody outer layers removed, thinly sliced
2 tsp ground coriander

Place the spice paste ingredients in a food processor and blend to a coarse paste. Pour half the paste into a large bowl and mix in the turmeric, a large pinch each of salt and pepper, half the lime juice and a splash of water. Add the chicken pieces, stir to coat and leave to marinate in the fridge for 30 minutes.

Heat 2 tablespoons of oil in a frying pan over a high heat and fry the curry leaves, kaffir lime leaves, lemongrass and spring onions until fragrant. Remove from the pan to a tray lined with paper towels to drain any excess oil. Set aside.

Heat another 2 tablespoons of oil in the pan over a medium heat and fry the remaining spice paste until fragrant, about 10–15 minutes, then add the remaining lime juice and season with salt and pepper to taste. Increase the heat to medium-high, add the chicken to the pan along with the fried spring onions, curry leaves and other aromatics and stir together. Continue stirring until the chicken is cooked through, about 5 minutes. Season and serve immediately.

GREEN CHILLI BRAISED DUCK
BEBEK CABAI HIJAU

I learnt how to cook this dish in Padang, Sumatra, where the fat of the duck skin is rendered over a charcoal fire. When making it in my small kitchen, I do this in a frying pan, which guarantees browned and crispy skin. The slow-cooking process mellows the heat and sharpness of the green chillies, which work beautifully with the duck.

The West Sumatrans love to eat Padang green chilli sambal with their dishes, so if you don't mind green chilli on top of green chilli (it's a bit like wearing double denim), I recommend going for it. It's lovely served with Turmeric yellow rice (p.247) and a side of vegetables.

Origin Padang, West Sumatra
Chilli heat Hot
Sambal suggestion Padang green chilli
    sambal (p.202)
Serves 4

---

4 skin-on, bone-in duck legs
2 bay leaves
2 kaffir lime leaves (optional)
Juice of ½ lime
Sea salt and black pepper, to taste

For the spice paste
2 lemongrass stalks, woody outer layers removed,
    thinly sliced
2 small banana shallots or 4 Thai shallots, peeled
    and sliced
7 garlic cloves, peeled and sliced
12 long green chillies (about 140g), sliced
2 spring onions (about 40g), white and light green
    parts only, sliced
Large handful of lemon basil, Thai basil or Italian
    basil leaves

Place the spice paste ingredients in a small food processor and blend to a semi-coarse paste.

Place the duck legs skin-side down in a large, deep ovenproof saucepan or cast-iron casserole with no oil. Place the pan over a medium-low heat for 10 minutes or until the skin is golden brown and crispy. Turn over the legs and cook the other side for 2 minutes. You may need to do this in batches, depending on the size of your pan. (If cooking in batches, after the first batch, decant any rendered duck fat into a jug, rinse out the pan and cook the remaining duck legs.) Remove the duck legs from the pan and set aside, reserving the rendered fat.

Preheat the oven to 180°C/160°C fan/gas 4. Increase the heat under the pan to medium and add the spice paste with the rendered duck fat, bay leaves and kaffir lime leaves, if using, then cook for 10–15 minutes. Pour 800ml cold water into the pan, then add the duck legs and bring to a simmer.

Cover with a lid, transfer the pan to the oven and cook for 1½ hours or until the duck is tender. Remove the duck from the pan, transfer to a board and let it rest, covered in foil, for 15 minutes.

Return the pan with the green chilli sauce to the hob on a high heat, stirring occasionally until the sauce is reduced, about 10–15 minutes. Season with the lime juice, salt and pepper. Arrange the duck legs on individual plates, pour over the sauce and serve immediately.

EGG CREPE ROLLS
SOSE SOLO

This healthier alternative to spring rolls is inspired by a dish made famous in Solo, central Java. I make it with chicken or pork, but you can use strips of stir-fried vegetables or any other filling of your choosing. *Sose solo* is a light dish that works well served in halves as canapés or snacks, or as a light starter. Egg crepes only work flawlessly in a small, good-quality non-stick pan – I use a 20cm pan. The filling will keep for up to 3 days in the fridge, but the egg crepes are best eaten on the day.

Origin Solo, Java
Chilli heat Moderate
Makes 15 (serves 6–8 as a starter)

60g dried rice vermicelli or other thin noodles
250g chicken or pork mince
100g shiitake, brown or chestnut mushrooms, stems removed, sliced
1 small pak choi (or similar green vegetable), finely chopped
Pinch of sea salt
2 garlic cloves, peeled and thinly sliced
2 spring onions, thinly sliced on the diagonal
¼ tsp ground nutmeg
Large pinch of ground white pepper
Large pinch of palm sugar or brown sugar
3 tbsp light soy sauce
2 tbsp kecap manis (p.254)
Juice of ½ lime
Coconut oil or sunflower oil, for frying
1 quantity of Sulawesi rica-rica chilli sauce (p.209), to serve

For the egg crepes
3 tbsp plain flour
Large pinch of sea salt
6 eggs, beaten

To make the crepes, sift the flour and salt into a mixing bowl. In a separate bowl, beat the eggs with 6 tablespoons of water. Gradually whisk the beaten eggs into the flour, 2 tablespoons at a time, until smooth. Pass through a sieve to remove any lumps.

Pour boiling water over the noodles and leave for 10 minutes (or follow the packet instructions). Drain and toss with a little oil to prevent them from sticking. Set aside.

Place a non-stick frying pan over a medium-low heat, add ½ teaspoon of oil, then wipe it out with a paper towel. Pour in 2 tablespoons of batter and swirl it around to very thinly coat the oiled pan. Smooth it with a teaspoon, if needed, and add extra batter to fill any holes. Cook for about 15 seconds on one side, then carefully flip it over to cook the other side. Repeat until you have used up all the batter. Stack the crepes and cover with foil.

Heat 2 tablespoons of oil in a wok or frying pan over a high heat, add the chicken or pork mince and fry, stirring, until well browned. Add the mushrooms and pak choi with the salt and cook for 2 minutes. Add the garlic and spring onions and cook for 1 minute, then add the nutmeg, white pepper and sugar. Return the noodles to the pan and stir through. Season with the soy sauce, kecap manis and lime juice and stir well. Add more salt or sugar to season, if needed.

To fill and roll the crepes, place a crepe flat on a chopping board and spread a spoonful of the mince and noodle mixture over the bottom third of the crepe, taking care not to overfill it. Fold in the left and right sides so it covers the edge of the filling, then roll up the crepe from the bottom to the top, just as you would for a spring roll. Repeat to fill and roll all the crepes. Cut each crepe roll in half on the diagonal and serve with the rica-rica chilli sauce to dip.

FRIED SPICED SOFT-BOILED EGGS
TELUR BUMBU MERAH

My grandmother Popo cooked these soft-boiled eggs for my mother whenever she came to visit and my aunty Tje Ie in Kupang has since taught me the recipe. The soft-boiled eggs are peeled and then deep-fried in hot oil, giving the exterior a wrinkled, pock-marked appearance that is textured and crispy. If you start with a soft-boiled egg you will get a custardy yolk in the centre which, together with the fragrant spice of the sauce, makes for a delicious meal. Serve with a side of vegetables and Coconut rice (p.246), if you like.

——

Origin Kupang, Timor
Chilli heat Mild
Serves 4 as a light lunch

——

8 eggs, soft-boiled for 6 minutes and peeled
Sea salt, to taste
Sunflower oil, for frying

For the spice paste
4 candlenuts or macadamia nuts (or 8 almonds or cashews)
2 tbsp coriander seeds
6 long red chillies, deseeded and sliced
4 garlic cloves, peeled and sliced
2 small banana shallots or 4 Thai shallots, peeled and sliced
2 tbsp palm sugar or brown sugar
1½ tbsp light soy sauce

To make the spice paste, place the nuts in a dry frying pan over a medium heat. Toast until golden, about 5 minutes. Add the coriander seeds and reduce the heat to low, then toast until fragrant. Place the toasted nuts and coriander seeds with the chillies, garlic and shallots in a small food processor and blend to a semi-coarse texture.

Heat 2 tablespoons of oil in a pan over a medium heat. Add the spice paste and fry for 10–15 minutes until softened and fragrant. Stir in the sugar, soy sauce and 2 tablespoons of water.

Fill a deep saucepan one-third full with oil and heat to 160ºC. (If you do not have a kitchen thermometer, check the oil is at temperature by adding a cube of bread; it should turn golden in 25–30 seconds.) Deep-fry the peeled, soft-boiled eggs until golden on the outside, then transfer to a tray lined with paper towels and season with salt. (Alternatively, if you do not want to deep-fry the eggs, you can pan-fry them with oil. They won't crisp up like the deep-fried version, but will still be delicious and warmed through.)

In a clean frying pan or wok, warm the deep-fried eggs and spice paste together. Serve immediately.

MEAT

—

With the largest Muslim population in the world, for whom eating pork is prohibited, beef, buffalo and goat are prized meats in Indonesia. Offal is considered both a delicacy and an economic necessity, echoing a nose-to-tail philosophy present all over the country. Hop over a few islands to the Hindu paradise of Bali, however, or to the volcanic Christian town of Manado in North Sulawesi, or to any of the Chinese-Indonesian communities spread across Indonesia, and you'll find an abundance of pork, known as *babi*. Pork belly is simmered in a kecap manis and chilli-spiced sauce, both fragrant and sweet, to form the delicious caramelised *babi kecap* (p.175); stir-fried pork belly marinated in coriander seeds, palm sugar and light soy sauce is the star of the Chinese-influenced noodle dish *kwetiau* (p.184); and I adore the spicy green chilli-laden *tinoransak* from North Sulawesi (p.179), which is fragrant with lemongrass and lemon basil stir-fried with thin slices of pork tenderloin.

Perhaps the dish that Indonesia is best known for is rendang, a spiced and caramelised dry coconut curry served with tender cubes of beef or buffalo. It has become a symbol of the movement of the Minangkabau people of Padang, West Sumatra, who are famed for their migration to other parts of the archipelago. The spices and aromatics that form the base of most Indonesian meat dishes act as a natural preservative, keeping the food safe to eat for days, and in some cases weeks. Mothers prepare large batches of rendang, which is then wrapped in banana leaf and taken away by their children as a constant reminder of home.

My travels through West Sumatra led me to a small village that lay on the outskirts of Padang, where I met the family of Pak Budi, a local taxi driver whose family offered to teach me their recipe for beef rendang (p.166). Due to its high price, beef is typically reserved for celebrations and to honour guests. Knowing this, the invitation to Pak's home was a privilege. His home was a bricolage of mismatched and harmonious materials that he had proudly amassed and built himself, including a small, basic kitchen with two woks, a sink and utility knives for cutting. Crouching elegantly on the concrete floor, for there were no tables and Pak had no use for one, Pak's mother Grandma Erneti began our lesson by preparing the spice paste, a mix of galangal, ginger, turmeric, shallots, garlic, candlenuts and chilli. Frying the ground spices together in the wok to release their fragrance, she added beef shin, coconut milk, kaffir lime leaf, bruised lemongrass and salam (Indonesian bay leaf) and left the rendang to simmer. After a couple of hours, she turned the heat to high and used the movement of her whole body to stir the ingredients until a thick, caramelised sauce, as intense and dark as tapenade, clung to the tenderised chunks of beef, which we all ate together sitting on the concrete floor.

In my own family, beef and coconut are a celebrated combination. My grandmother Popo's coconut beef and peanut stir-fry (p.170) is quick, warming and comforting. Thin slices of beef are seared and combined with crunchy peanuts and coconut, brought together by a rich chilli, tomato and tamarind sauce. In barbecue weather, our family's soy and ginger beef satay (p.169) goes on the grill: luscious chunks of tender beef marinated and charred to form a caramelised crust and served with peanut sauce (p.204) or sambal, a much-loved combination in Indonesia.

In this chapter there's a good mix of easy-to-whip-up dishes that can be cooked with only a handful of ingredients, as well as celebration dishes that require a little bit of effort. Take note that the Indonesian way of cooking meat will require you to throw all your culinary techniques out the window. Meat is rarely browned in a pan before being thrown into a stew, and Indonesians don't typically marinate meat overnight. Many households were without refrigeration until recently, meaning a long marinade time was not possible. The traditional Indonesian home cook will marinate their meat for less than an hour, as the complexity in these dishes is achieved by releasing the fragrance in the spice paste, but I have made suggestions where a longer marinade will benefit the flavour. Invest in the best-quality meat you can afford, as it will make a difference to the finished dish. The recipes here form a small introduction to the wonderful flavours that stretch from the east of Indonesia to the west – but they are a carefully curated selection of dishes that capture the heart of Indonesian soul cooking: comfort food that gives a reason to celebrate.

BEEF RENDANG
RENDANG DAGING

I've learnt to cook rendang from several culinary greats, including my mentor Sri Owen and Indonesian chef William Wongso, as well as home cooks met on my travels. There are many interpretations of rendang, but the traditional definition is a slow-cooked dry beef curry that starts in a bath of white coconut milk and finishes a near-black colour when the oil splits from the milk and caramelises the beef. The result is beef that is crispy on the outside and melt-in-the-mouth tender on the inside, laden with roasted tropical spices and creamy, caramelised coconut.

This recipe is my nod to all these wonderful traditional cooks, taking an idea from one and blending it with another to produce what I believe to be a fantastic representation of rendang from the region. Serve it with a heap of Turmeric yellow rice (p.247) to soak up the sauce, Padang green chilli sambal and a side of Asian greens. The cooking technique of rendang preserves the beef, so Sri Owen has always proudly stated it can last several days in the fridge, or 3 months in the freezer. It can be reheated in the microwave or in the oven at 150°C/130°C fan/gas 2, covered in foil.

Origin Padang, West Sumatra
Chilli heat Moderate
Sambal suggestion Padang green chilli sambal (p.202)
Serves 4

———

1kg braising beef, such as shin or brisket, trimmed of fat
800ml coconut milk
1 tsp sea salt
2 lemongrass stalks, bruised and tied in a knot
3 bay leaves
5 kaffir lime leaves (optional)

For the spice paste

7 long red chillies, sliced (deseeded if you prefer less heat)
3 small banana shallots or 6 Thai shallots, peeled and sliced
5 garlic cloves, peeled and sliced
8cm piece of ginger (about 40g), peeled and sliced
8cm piece of galangal (about 40g), woody stem removed, thinly sliced (optional)
3cm piece of fresh turmeric (about 15g), peeled and sliced (or 1 tsp ground turmeric)
2 tsp ground coriander
1 tsp ground cumin

———

Place the spice paste ingredients in a small food processor and blend to a smooth paste. If the texture is too coarse, add a splash of the measured coconut milk and blend again.

Cut the beef into 3–4cm chunks, removing any excess fat. Do not cut the chunks too small or the beef will disintegrate during the cooking process. Place the spice paste in a deep, heavy-based

Continues overleaf

saucepan along with the beef, coconut milk, salt, lemongrass, bay leaves and kaffir lime leaves, if using. Bring to the boil, then reduce to a gentle simmer, stirring every 20 minutes to ensure the rendang doesn't stick to the base of the pan.

After 2–2½ hours, the oil from the coconut milk will split and rise to the surface, appearing as a reddish-orange oil – Indonesians call this stage 'kalio'. Depending on the oil content of your coconut milk, this may be a subtle film of oil or there can be a pool of it. Remove the lemongrass stalks – if they cook any further, they may disintegrate and be impossible to remove.

Turn the heat up to medium-high to reduce the sauce. Stir the rendang continuously until the sauce has thickened and turned a deep brown. As more oil separates, you are nearly there. Continue stirring the beef so it absorbs the sauce and caramelises on the outside. Taste and adjust the seasoning if needed before serving.

Variation: Tofu and boiled egg rendang

You can easily make a vegetarian rendang. Make the sauce following the steps in the recipe above, omitting the beef. Simmer the sauce and take it to the kalio stage, where the oil separates. Reduce the sauce to your preferred consistency and then add 6 whole, peeled soft-boiled eggs and 300g firm tofu, cut into cubes. Squeeze any excess moisture from the tofu using paper towels before adding it. Warm everything together, but don't try to caramelise the eggs or tofu or they will fall apart. Serve immediately.

Variation: Rendang toasties

These toasties are brilliant to make if you have any leftover rendang and own a sandwich toaster. Using a basic sliced loaf, simply butter the outside of 2 slices of bread, turn them over and fill one side with the leftover rendang. Make the sandwich and then place in the sandwich toaster until the toastie is golden on the outside.

SOY AND GINGER BEEF SATAY
SATE DAGING

Within our family, there is a great tradition of making satay, which gives my father his reputation as the barbecue king. The smoky, charred marinade that coats the tender cubes of meat in this recipe is always a reminder of my childhood summers when we would grill satay over hot coals in the back garden with the scorching sun above us. The beautiful flavours of garlic, ginger and soy combine in the marinade to make this satay a showstopper for any occasion, but particularly satisfying to eat on a summer day. Served with the peanut sauce or shallot sambal, I am transported to Indonesia every time I take a bite.

I like my beef a little on the pinker side, so try to get a good sear to brown the meat until it is just cooked through. Marinating the meat for up to a day in advance gives the best results. I like to eat it with Fried shallot and coconut rice (p.76) or stir-fried vegetables.

Origin Popular all over Indonesia
Chilli heat Mild or hot, depending on the sambal
Serves 6 as a starter or 4 as a light main

———

800g lean beef steak (such as sirloin, rump or ribeye), cut into 2–3cm cubes
2 quantities of Caramelised shallot sambal bawang (p.200) or Peanut sauce (p.204), to serve
Sunflower oil, for grilling

For the marinade
120ml light soy sauce
60ml rice vinegar or white wine vinegar
4cm (about 20g) ginger, peeled and grated
4 garlic cloves, peeled and crushed
2 tsp palm sugar or brown sugar
1 tsp ground coriander
2 tbsp sesame oil

———

You will need 12 wooden skewers, soaked in water for at least 30 minutes before cooking.

Combine the ingredients for the marinade in a large bowl. Add the cubes of beef, toss until thoroughly coated and leave to marinate in the fridge for at least 2 hours, but preferably overnight.

When ready to cook, thread about 5 cubes of beef onto each skewer.

Oil a griddle or barbecue and turn the heat to high. Cook the beef skewers for 1–2 minutes on each side or until done to your liking. Serve immediately, drizzled with the sambal or peanut sauce and with any remaining sauce in a bowl on the side.

COCONUT BEEF AND PEANUT STIR-FRY
SERUNDENG DAGING

This recipe spans three generations of my family, beginning when my grandmother Popo made it in Timor for her four children. It's a dish that reminds my father of his island home, where Popo seared the beef on the 100-year-old wok that my aunty Tje Ie still uses today. The crunch of peanuts and aroma of grated coconut are typical of the Indonesian cuisine that he loves, combined with the heat and spice of the chilli and the punchy flavours of the sauce. This is a very quick stir-fry that is heavenly to eat and incredibly easy to rustle up. I like to eat it with a simple side of white rice and vegetables.

___

Origin Kupang, Timor
Chilli heat Hot
Serves 4

___

600g sirloin, rump or ribeye steak, sliced on an
    angle against the grain
4 kaffir lime leaves or 2 bay leaves
50g unsweetened desiccated coconut
120g unsalted roasted peanuts, roughly chopped
3 tsp tamarind paste (or 3 tsp lime juice mixed
    with 3 tsp brown sugar)
Sea salt and black pepper, to taste
Coconut oil or sunflower oil, for frying

For the marinade
1½ tbsp light soy sauce
½ tbsp rice vinegar or white wine vinegar
1 tbsp sunflower oil
1 tsp cornflour

For the spice paste
4 small banana shallots or 8 Thai shallots, peeled
    and sliced
12 long red chillies, sliced
8 garlic cloves, peeled and sliced
4 tomatoes, quartered

Take the meat out of the fridge 30 minutes before cooking to allow it to come to room temperature. Combine the marinade ingredients in a bowl and massage it into the meat. Set aside to marinate for a minimum of 15 minutes.

Place the spice paste ingredients in a small food processor and blend to a semi-coarse paste.

Add 2 tablespoons of oil to a frying pan or large wok over a medium heat and fry the spice paste with the kaffir lime leaves or bay leaves until fragrant, about 15 minutes. Remove from the wok and set aside.

Meanwhile, place the desiccated coconut in a separate pan over a medium heat. Toast the coconut in the pan until golden brown all over, then set aside.

Heat 1 tablespoon of oil in the pan over a high heat and, when the oil is shimmering, stir-fry the beef in batches for a couple of minutes at a time or until it is well browned, adding more oil if necessary.

Return the spice paste to the pan with the peanuts, toasted coconut and beef and add a splash of water so that the spice paste loosely hugs the meat (add more water if needed). Warm it through, stirring well to combine. Season to taste with the tamarind, salt and pepper. Transfer to a serving platter and serve immediately.

STICKY BEEF SHORT RIB WITH CHILLI
IGA BUMBU DENDENG BALADO

This beef short rib recipe benefits from low and slow cooking in the oven, resulting in meltingly tender chunks of meat, seared to a deep brown on the outside and then bathed in a divine sticky sauce of dates, kecap manis, coriander and Indonesian spices. It's the perfect celebration dish for dinner parties. The traditional *dendeng balado* is Indonesia's answer to beef jerky, for which the meat is marinated, boiled and then deep-fried, a style famous in Padang, which must be chewed with full force to counter its toughness! I've adapted the recipe, using all the flavours of the marinade but preserving the tenderness and juiciness of the beef.

Balado means 'with chillies' and this dish is served with a simple combination of red chillies and lime juice that balances the richness of the short rib sauce. If you can't find short ribs in your supermarket, you can use any cut of beef that lends itself well to slow cooking, such as beef cheeks, shin or braising steak. Serve it with mashed potatoes and green vegetables. It will keep for up to 3 days in the fridge.

Origin Padang, West Sumatra
Chilli heat Hot
Serves 4

———

1.15kg beef short rib on the bone (roughly 4 individual short ribs)
3 tbsp tamarind paste (or 3 tbsp lime juice mixed with 3 tbsp brown sugar)
2 tbsp rice vinegar or white wine vinegar
4 tbsp kecap manis (p.254)
4 tbsp light soy sauce
4 tbsp palm sugar or brown sugar
Sea salt and black pepper, to taste
Coconut oil or sunflower oil, for frying

For the spice paste
3 garlic cloves, peeled and sliced
5cm piece of ginger (about 25g), peeled and sliced
2 long red chillies, sliced
2 small banana shallots or 4 Thai shallots, peeled and sliced
6 dates, stones removed, sliced
2 tsp ground coriander

For the balado sauce
10 long red chillies, half deseeded, all thinly sliced
4 small banana shallots or 8 Thai shallots, peeled and thinly sliced
3 kaffir lime leaves (optional), stems removed, thinly sliced
Large pinch each of salt and black pepper
Juice of 1–2 limes

———

Preheat the oven to 150ºC/130ºC fan/gas 2. Place the spice paste ingredients in a small food processor with a splash of water and blend to a smooth paste. Add 2 tablespoons of oil to a frying

Continues overleaf

pan over a medium heat and fry the spice paste for 10–15 minutes or until fragrant. Transfer to a deep roasting tray and set aside.

Pat the beef dry and season with salt and black pepper. Wipe clean the frying pan and then heat 2 tablespoons of oil in the pan over a high heat. When the oil begins to shimmer, add the meat and brown for about 1–2 minutes on each side, until nicely seared and well browned.

Mix the cooked spice paste with 210ml water, the tamarind, vinegar, kecap manis, soy and sugar in the roasting tray and add the seared beef, ensuring it is halfway submerged. Top up with more water if needed. Cover the tray with foil and roast in the oven for 3–3½ hours until the beef is tender and falling off the bone.

Meanwhile, prepare the balado sauce. Heat 2 tablespoons of oil in a frying pan over a medium heat and fry the chilli, shallots and kaffir lime leaves together until softened. Season with the salt, pepper and lime juice. You are looking for a punchy, sharp sauce to balance the richness of the beef.

When cooked, let the beef rest for 10 minutes before serving. While the beef is resting, reduce the short rib sauce in a pan over a high heat until thickened and slightly caramelised. Season the sauce with salt, if needed. Serve the beef with a generous helping of the sticky sauce and the balado sauce on the side.

———

Variation: Quick dendeng

If you're short of time, substitute the short rib of beef for sirloin or rump steak. Season with salt, pepper and oil and pan fry the steak to your liking. You will not need the spice paste for this recipe, just serve with the balado sauce.

SWEET SOY PORK BELLY
BABI KECAP

This dish was a regular feature at our dinner table when I was growing up, and I used to ask my grandmother Popo to make it for me all the time. It is infused with the flavours of lemongrass, ginger, galangal, chilli, and the sweet, molasses-like kecap manis broth which reduces into a luscious, sticky sauce that caramelises and clings to the cubes of tender pork belly. Best served with Brown rice (p.245) and a side of steamed greens. The pork keeps well for up to 3 days in the fridge.

——

Origin Bali
Chilli heat Moderate
Sambal suggestion Fresh Balinese sambal matah (p.206)
Serves 4

——

2 lemongrass stalks, bruised and tied in a knot
2 bay leaves
75ml kecap manis (p.254)
Coconut oil or sunflower oil, for frying

For the pork
1 tsp ground nutmeg
2 tsp ground coriander
1 tsp ground white pepper
1 tsp ground black pepper
¼ tsp sea salt
½ tsp palm sugar or brown sugar
500g skinless, boneless pork belly, cut into 2cm chunks

For the spice paste
8 garlic cloves, peeled and sliced
2 small banana shallots or 4 Thai shallots, peeled and sliced
4 long red chillies, sliced
10cm piece of ginger (about 50g), peeled and sliced
6cm piece of galangal (about 30g), woody stem removed, sliced (optional)

——

Combine the nutmeg, coriander, white and black pepper, salt and sugar in a large bowl. Add the pork, toss to coat it thoroughly and leave to marinate for 15 minutes.

Place the spice paste ingredients in a small food processor and blend to a smooth paste.

Heat 2 tablespoons of oil in a deep pan over a medium heat and add the spice paste, along with the lemongrass and bay leaves. Fry the paste until fragrant, about 10 minutes, then add the pork, searing it lightly as the meat combines with the spice paste. After a few minutes, add the kecap manis and 200ml water and bring to the boil. Lower the heat and simmer for 30–45 minutes or until the sauce is reduced and caramelised, and the pork is tender.

——

Variation: Vegan sweet soy aubergine

You can make this recipe vegan by replacing the pork with 2 large aubergines cut into 3cm cubes. Cook the aubergine following the pork recipe above, coating the aubergine chunks with the spice paste first, before adding the kecap manis and water. Simmer for 30–45 minutes or until the aubergine is soft and the sauce is reduced and caramelised.

BALINESE STICKY GLAZED PORK RIBS
IGA BABI BALI

Barbecued pork ribs is one of the most popular dishes in Bali: a smoky, juicy and tender meat feast that is glazed in sweet and sticky kecap manis and grilled over charcoal. You would be hard pressed not to be drawn to Bali's barbecue restaurants, with their grills strategically placed at each entrance to fill the pavements with the aroma of the marinade.

This version is slow cooked in a kecap manis, ginger, garlic and chilli marinade that is caramelised under the grill to produce an irresistibly sticky rack of ribs. It can be made in advance and reheated, making it a great choice for a dinner party. It will keep for up to 3 days in the fridge; reheat it in the oven at 170°C/150°C fan/gas 3 for 10 minutes, covered with foil. I love to serve the ribs with sweet potato wedges or Fragrant stir-fried morning glory (p.100) and Fried shallot and coconut rice (p.76).

Origin Bali
Chilli heat Moderate
Serves 4–6

———

8 long red chillies, roughly chopped (deseeded if you prefer less heat)
12 garlic cloves, peeled and roughly chopped
12cm piece of ginger (about 60g), peeled and roughly chopped
2 small banana shallots or 4 Thai shallots, peeled and roughly chopped
120ml rice vinegar or white wine vinegar
140ml kecap manis (p.254)
100g palm sugar or brown sugar
1 tsp sea salt flakes
2 x 700g racks of pork spare ribs

———

Preheat the oven to 170°C/150°C fan/gas 3. Blend all the ingredients except the pork with 120ml water in a food processor until smooth.

Line a roasting tin with four long layers of foil in the shape of a cross – two horizontal and two vertical – with enough excess foil spilling over the sides to wrap the ribs. Lay the ribs onto the foil and pour over half the marinade, massaging it into each rack. Wrap the ribs with the foil and roast in the oven on the top or middle shelf for 2 hours.

While the ribs are roasting, pour the remaining marinade into a small saucepan and bring to the boil. Reduce the heat and simmer the sauce until it has thickened, roughly 5–10 minutes. Remove from the heat and set aside.

To check if the ribs are done, test an end rib – when you tug the end bone, the meat should start slipping off the bone. If they are not yet tender,

Continues overleaf

return to the oven and test again after 10 minutes. Once the ribs have finished roasting, remove from the oven and turn the grill to high. Open the foil and brush some of the reduced marinade onto the ribs, reserving the rest as a dipping sauce. Place the ribs under the grill for 5–7 minutes, uncovered, until they darken in colour and the marinade caramelises. Serve immediately, with the remaining marinade in a dipping bowl.

———

Variation: Vegan butternut ribs

You can make a vegan version using butternut squash, which will serve 6.

Preheat the oven to 220°C/200°C fan/gas 7. Peel 2 butternut squash and cut in half lengthways. Scoop out the seeds and cut the squash widthways into rib-like wedges that are 2cm thick.

Spread out the butternut slices on an oiled flat baking tray (you may need 2 trays to fit all the slices on) and season very lightly with salt and pepper. Halve 2 whole garlic bulbs and nestle the halves alongside the squash on the tray. Roast for 30 minutes in the hot oven, turning the slices halfway through cooking.

Prepare the marinade as described in the main recipe, halving the ingredient quantities and reducing in a small saucepan for 5–10 minutes. Preheat the grill to high. Remove the tray from the oven, spoon a little of the marinade on top of each slice of squash and place under the grill for up to 5 minutes, or until the squash takes on a little colour. Keep an eye on it while it is grilling, as the slices can very quickly catch and burn. Discard the garlic, then serve the squash immediately with rice, greens and the rest of the marinade as a dipping sauce on the side.

GREEN CHILLI AND LEMONGRASS PORK
TINORANSAK

As I travelled the region, I came across this famed dish from Manado on the island of Sulawesi time after time. It very quickly became a staple I would order whenever I saw it on a restaurant menu. *Tinoransak* is a fresh-tasting stir-fry scented with lemongrass and lemon basil, made zesty from the lime juice squeezed over it just before serving. Don't be put off by the high number of chillies in this recipe; the resulting flavour gives a medium heat, as the burn of the chilli is cooked out in the spice paste.

The traditional version is served with pork, a favoured meat in the Christian region of North Sulawesi, but it could easily be substituted with strips of chicken. If you're looking to make this dish vegetarian, replace the pork with mushrooms, such as shiitake, oyster or Portobello, or cubes of firm tofu or tempeh.

It's good with Coconut rice (p.246) and a side of the refreshing Sulawesi sambal *dabu-dabu*. *Tinoransak* will keep for up to 2 days in the fridge.

Origin Manado, Sulawesi
Chilli heat Moderate
Sambal suggestion Fresh tomato and basil dabu-dabu (p.196)
Serves 4

---

2 kaffir lime leaves or 1 bay leaf
600g pork fillet tenderloin, thinly sliced
Juice of 2 limes, plus extra to taste
25g bunch of lemon basil, Thai basil or Italian basil, leaves only
Sea salt and white or black pepper, to taste
Coconut oil or sunflower oil, for frying

For the spice paste
200g (about 16) long green chillies, sliced (deseeded if you prefer less heat)
3 small banana shallots or 6 Thai shallots, peeled and sliced
14 garlic cloves, peeled and sliced
7cm piece of ginger (about 35g), peeled and sliced
6cm piece of galangal (about 30g), woody stem removed, sliced (or another 6cm ginger)
2 lemongrass stalks, woody outer layers removed, thinly sliced

---

Place all the spice paste ingredients in a food processor and pulse to a coarse paste – it's important for the flavour that it isn't too smooth.

Heat 2 tablespoons of oil in a frying pan over a medium heat, add the spice paste and kaffir lime leaves or bay leaf and sauté for about 10–15 minutes until fragrant.

Add the pork and stir together with the spice paste, cooking until the pork is no longer pink. Add the lime juice and a splash of water and place a lid on the frying pan, reducing the heat to a simmer. Continue cooking until the liquid is reduced and clinging to the ingredients, then stir through the basil leaves, reserving a few for garnish. Season with salt, pepper and a little more lime if needed. Serve immediately, garnished with fresh basil leaves.

BALINESE ROASTED PORK BELLY
BABI GULING

My spiced pork belly is inspired by the *babi guling* found all over Bali, where queues for open-fire rotisseries appear every day. Suckling pigs are painstakingly skewered by hand and rubbed inside and out with an aromatic spice paste, then rotated slowly over a fire made from the fragrant branches of a coffee tree. The pigs are turned by strong, relentless hands for five hours amidst searing heat and clouds of spiced smoke until their skin is crisp, crackled and browned.

This adapted recipe calls only for an oven, but is still a dish worthy of a celebratory Sunday roast. The slow-cooking method guarantees succulent meat with crispy crackling, and the spices are reminiscent of the flavours of Bali. After hours of oven roasting, the spice paste absorbs the pork fat, making a decadent sauce that replaces any need for gravy. Serve with roasted potatoes and Fragrant stir-fried morning glory (p.100), or any vegetable accompaniments that suit a roast. The meat benefits from being marinated overnight to absorb the flavours of the spice paste, but if you're short of time, it's still tasty without any marinating at all. It's best eaten on the day but will keep for 3 days in the fridge. Reheat the pork in the oven, wrapped in foil, at 180°C/160°C fan/gas 4.

Pictured overleaf

Origin Bali
Chilli heat Moderate
Sambal suggestion Fresh Balinese sambal matah (p.206)
Serves 4

──

1.5kg skin-on, boneless pork belly
5 kaffir lime leaves (optional), stalks removed, thinly sliced
2 bay leaves, stalks removed, thinly sliced
Sea salt, to taste
Coconut oil or sunflower oil, for the skin and for frying

For the spice paste
12cm piece of ginger (about 60g), peeled and sliced
12cm piece of galangal (about 60g), woody stem removed, sliced (optional)
18 garlic cloves, peeled and sliced
6 candlenuts or macadamia nuts (or 8 almonds or cashew nuts), toasted for best flavour
6 small banana shallots or 12 Thai shallots, peeled and sliced
9 long red chillies, sliced (deseeded if you prefer less heat)
6cm piece of fresh turmeric (about 30g), peeled and sliced (or 2 tsp ground turmeric)
¾ tsp ground nutmeg
1½ tsp ground white pepper
1½ tsp ground black pepper
3 tsp ground coriander
¾ tsp sea salt

Pat the pork belly skin dry with a paper towel. Using a sharp knife, score the skin with lines that are 1–2cm apart, taking care to cut a few millimetres into the fat below the skin, but not into the meat.

Place all the spice paste ingredients in a food processor and blend to a semi-smooth texture. Mix together with the sliced kaffir lime leaves and bay leaves.

Wearing gloves to prevent staining from the turmeric, place the pork skin-side down on the chopping board and rub some spice paste into the flesh. Place the remaining spice paste in the centre of a deep roasting tray and lay the flesh side of the pork on top. Chill the pork in the fridge, uncovered, for at least 2 hours or preferably overnight – this helps the skin to dry out.

When you are ready to cook, preheat the oven to 180°C/160°C fan/gas 4. Remove the pork from the fridge 30 minutes before cooking to allow it to come to room temperature. Pat the skin dry to remove any excess moisture, then rub it all over with a little oil and a couple of pinches of salt, ensuring the salt gets into the scored lines. Check that the spice paste is neatly packed underneath the pork belly so it's protected while cooking.

Roast the pork in the oven for 2 hours, then remove the tray from the oven and turn the temperature up to 220°C/200°C fan/gas 7. Place the pork belly on a chopping board. Remove as much of the spice paste from the tray as possible (it will burn if cooked at the higher temperature), transfer to a bowl and set aside – it should be nicely combined with the melted pork fat.

Return the pork belly to the tray and cook for a further 30 minutes. Finally, increase the temperature to 240°C/220°C fan/gas 9 and cook the pork for another 20–30 minutes, or until the skin has completely crackled. Remove from the oven and rest for 15 minutes. (If parts of the crackling start to burn during cooking, turn the tray around and cover the burnt sections with foil to ensure they don't darken any further.)

While the pork rests, add 1 tablespoon of oil to a frying pan over a medium-high heat and add the spice paste reserved from the tray. Cook the spice paste for 10–15 minutes until nicely caramelised. Slice the pork into individual servings and ensure each plate gets a generous spoonful of the spice paste beside it.

183 Meat

PORK AND PRAWN RICE NOODLES
KWETIAU

I first tasted the Chinese-influenced dish of *kwetiau* in the city of Medan, North Sumatra, at the restaurant of Ibu Huey, a lady whose name means 'fire' in Chinese, and one which seems apt when watching the flames lick up the edge of her carbon-steel wok as she stir-fries. Standing in front of her restaurant in a leopard-print blouse and knickerbockers, she flash-fries to order, serving up steaming plates of flat rice noodles with slices of marinated pork, prawns and scrambled duck egg. A signature dish of Medan, this is one of my all-time favourite stir-fries, a dish I return to again and again.

——

Origin Medan, North Sumatra
Sambal suggestion Caramelised shallot sambal
    bawang (p.200)
Serves 2

——

200g skinless, boneless pork belly, cut into lardons
2 tbsp light soy sauce
2 tbsp palm sugar or brown sugar
2 tsp ground coriander
120g flat rice noodles (5mm thick), or other
    similar-shaped noodles
2 garlic cloves, peeled and very thinly sliced
120g raw king prawns, deveined and peeled but
    with tails left intact
2 duck or hen's eggs
1 large pak choi (or any green vegetable of your
    choice), chopped into small chunks
2 spring onions, thinly sliced on the diagonal
50g bean sprouts
Coconut oil or sunflower oil, for frying

For the marinade
2 tbsp light soy sauce
2 tbsp palm sugar or brown sugar
2 tsp ground coriander

Mix together the marinade ingredients to make a paste, then stir it through the pork lardons and set aside for 15 minutes. In a separate bowl, mix together the soy sauce, sugar and ground coriander and set aside.

Place the noodles in a heatproof bowl and pour boiling hot water over them so they are completely covered. Allow to soak for 10 minutes (or follow the packet instructions), then drain and run under cold water. Return the noodles to the bowl and toss with a little of the oil so they do not stick together.

Heat 1 tablespoon of oil in a wok or large frying pan over a high heat. When the oil is hot, add the pork lardons and marinade. Move the pork continuously around the pan for a few minutes until cooked through, then remove and set aside. Heat another tablespoon of oil in the pan, then add the garlic and prawns. Cook, stirring continuously, for 2 minutes or until the prawns have just turned pink, then remove from the pan and set aside.

Heat another tablespoon of oil in the pan over a high heat, add the noodles and cook for 1 minute, then move everything to one side. Add 1 teaspoon of oil and crack the eggs straight into the empty side of the pan. Leave the eggs to cook for a minute until beginning to set, continue cooking to scramble them, then stir them through the noodles. Return the prawns, garlic and pork lardons to the pan, along with the pak choi, spring onions, bean sprouts and prepared sauce. Cook for a further 2 minutes, stirring, until the prawns are cooked through and the pak choi has softened, then serve immediately.

CRISPY PORK BELLY INSTANT NOODLES
INDOMIE DENGAN BABI TORE

Indomie are dried instant noodles that cook in just 3 minutes. Beloved across Indonesia, they are eaten for breakfast, lunch, dinner and as a snack, served up by fast-food vendors in every flavour imaginable to anyone in need of comfort food.

The vinegar-marinated pork belly known as *babi tore* is a dish popular in Sulawesi and Timor. The meat is drizzled with vinegar and white pepper both before and after cooking to give its distinctive flavour. Crispy on the outside and juicy on the inside, when combined with the instant noodles it results in a delicious, flavour-packed meal.

Origin Kupang, Timor and Manado, Sulawesi
Chilli heat Hot
Sambal suggestion Sulawesi rica-rica chilli sauce (p.209)
Serves 4

For the marinated pork
3 tbsp rice vinegar or white wine vinegar, plus extra for drizzling
½ tsp ground white pepper, plus extra to taste
1 tsp sea salt
400g skinless, boneless pork belly, cut into lardons
Sunflower oil, for frying

For the noodles
4 x 100g packets of dried instant noodles (or dried thin egg or rice noodles)
120ml oyster sauce
2 tbsp fish sauce
4 tbsp kecap manis (p.254)
4 tbsp coconut oil or sunflower oil
8 long red chillies, thinly sliced (deseeded if you prefer less heat)
8 garlic cloves, peeled and crushed

300g greens such as pak choi, broccoli or kale, chopped into large chunks

To serve
Unsalted roasted peanuts, roughly chopped
Coriander leaves or Chinese celery leaves
Kerupuk (p.28) or prawn crackers

Put the vinegar, pepper and salt in a small bowl and stir to combine. Pour over the pork belly and leave to marinate for 15 minutes.

Add a generous layer of oil to a large frying pan or wok over a high heat. Once the oil starts to shimmer, add the pork belly in batches and fry until golden and crispy, adding more oil when necessary. Transfer to a tray lined with paper towels to absorb any excess oil. Tip the pork into a bowl and drizzle over a little extra vinegar and a sprinkle of white pepper.

Meanwhile, cook the noodles in boiling water according to the packet instructions, about 2–5 minutes. Do not use the seasoning included in the packets.

Mix the oyster sauce, fish sauce and kecap manis in a small bowl and set aside. Heat 2 tablespoons of the oil in a wok or large frying pan over a medium-high heat. Add half the chilli and stir-fry for 1 minute. Add half the crushed garlic and half the greens and stir-fry for a further 1 minute or until the greens are tender. Add 2 servings of the noodles, half of the pork and half of the kecap manis mixture. Stir together until well combined, then remove from the pan and keep warm. Repeat with the remaining ingredients.

Divide the noodles between serving bowls, then scatter over the peanuts and herb leaves. Serve with a side of crackers.

ACEHNESE LAMB CURRY
GULAI KAMBING ACEH

Gulai kambing is a rich, slow-braised goat or lamb curry flavoured with Indian-influenced spices typical of the city of Aceh in North Sumatra: turmeric, curry leaves, coriander, cumin, star anise and cinnamon. Typically eaten in the unrelenting humidity of Aceh, a refreshing iced tea alongside provides welcome respite. With tender chunks of meat and creamy spiced coconut milk, it is also pure comfort food on a winter's evening with Turmeric yellow rice (p.247) and vegetables.

This dish is served hot in Aceh, but if you prefer less heat, deseed half or all of the chillies.

———

Origin Aceh, North Sumatra
Chilli heat Hot
Serves 4

———

300ml coconut milk
2 tbsp tamarind paste (or 2 tbsp lime juice mixed with 2 tbsp brown sugar)
1kg lamb leg, lamb shoulder or goat leg, cut into 3cm chunks
Sea salt and white pepper, to taste
Coconut oil or sunflower oil, for frying

For the spice paste
4 candlenuts or macadamia nuts (or 8 almonds or cashews)
22 long red chillies (about 270g), sliced (deseeded if you prefer less heat)
6 garlic cloves, peeled and sliced
6 small banana shallots or 12 Thai shallots, peeled and sliced
5cm piece of fresh turmeric (about 25g), peeled and sliced (or 1½ tsp ground turmeric)
4cm piece of ginger (about 20g), peeled and sliced
2 tsp ground coriander
1 tsp ground cumin

For the aromatics
1 star anise
1 cinnamon stick
2 lemongrass stalks, bruised and tied in a knot
8 dried chillies
6 kaffir lime leaves (optional)
Handful of fresh or dried curry leaves (optional)
2 bay leaves

———

Place the star anise and cinnamon stick in a dry frying pan over a medium-low heat and toast until fragrant. Remove from the pan and set aside. Increase the heat to medium and toast the nuts in the same pan.

Place the toasted nuts in a food processor with the spice paste ingredients and blend until smooth.

Heat 3 tablespoons of oil in a deep, heavy-based pan over a medium heat. Add the spice paste and all the aromatics and stir until fragrant, about 10–15 minutes.

Add the coconut milk, tamarind paste and another 3 tablespoons of oil. Simmer to reduce the sauce for about 20 minutes, stirring every 2–3 minutes, until the oil separates from the spice paste. It may be subtle, but you will see a small film of oil leaching out from the edges of the sauce as you stir it, bubbling and frying on the base of the pan. You must stir the sauce frequently once the coconut milk has been added, otherwise it may burn.

Add the lamb or goat, a good pinch of salt and 500ml water, bring to the boil, then reduce the heat and simmer gently for 1½–2 hours, topping up the water a little if needed. Stir every 20 minutes or so to ensure it doesn't catch on the bottom.

The dish is ready when the meat is tender and juicy and the sauce thick and unctuous. Season with salt and pepper to taste, then serve.

SAMBAL

—

Sambal is a hot relish that originated in Java, Indonesia. There are thousands of versions across the archipelago, and sambal can also be found in Sri Lanka, Malaysia, Singapore and Brunei. The term derives from the Javanese word *sambel*, meaning 'condiment', and for most Indonesians a meal is not complete without it.

Nearly every meal is built around sambal, which is placed in the centre of the table along with rice and *kerupuk* crackers; meat, fish and vegetable dishes surround sambal as supporting acts, rather than the main event. At the heart of any sambal recipe are fresh or dried chillies, enhanced with flavours that may include (but are not limited to) garlic, ginger, lemongrass, tomatoes, citrus and *terasi* (fermented shrimp paste). The traditional Indonesian home cook grinds their sambal using a heavy *cobek* and *ulekan*, a version of the mortar and pestle that can be made of hard wood or volcanic rock, such as granite. They work the *ulekan* (pestle) back and forth, sliding it across the *cobek* using the weight of their body to crush the ingredients to a gleaming paste. Happily, even the most authentic Indonesian chefs appreciate a shortcut. I have watched legendary Indonesian cookery writer Sri Owen make her sambal using a food processor, so I now use my food processor with a clear conscience when batch-cooking sambal – it takes no time at all to make and still tastes delicious.

I learnt to love and appreciate spicy food from an early age, perhaps thanks to the influence of my grandmother Popo. Now there is always a healthy supply of sambal in my fridge and my freezer, which finds its way into soups, onto eggs and to accompany any dishes or snacks to which the sultry heat of sambal can lend itself. Sambal is a very personal dish, with each region having its own variation and every family their own recipe. Indonesians can get quite nostalgic about sambal – it reminds them of home.

My quest to learn about sambal led me to a dimly lit kitchen in Ubud at the home of a Balinese ceremony chef called Pak Darta, a quiet man who dresses in traditional batik-patterned clothing and is famed on the island for cooking feasts for up to 800 guests at funerals, marriages and births. In his kitchen, Pak Darta prepared the ingredients for our first sambal. Waving his hand over a woven basket filled with spices, he picked up the galangal. 'This one is good to rub on itchy skin,' he said in a mix of broken English and Bahasa Indonesian, before moving on to the turmeric, 'for cuts,' and then the multi-purpose ginger, 'for when your blood is not running well.' He also told me it's good for smelly armpits, pointing to his underarms. What I soon came to realise is that the ingredients in Indonesian spice pastes and sambals also contain natural remedies to promote good health and cure ailments. Together we made sambal matah (p.206), a raw sambal made of sliced shallot, chilli, garlic and kaffir lime, and sambal tomat (p.194), a cooked sambal of ground chilli, garlic, shallot, ginger and tomato, which works beautifully as a condiment and marinade.

While sambal must balance heat, saltiness, sweetness and sourness, another essential element is umami. In its simplest form, umami can be described as a savoury flavour – the fifth taste sensation. It is that moment when all flavours are in perfect harmony, in the same way that Parmesan can elevate a humble pasta dish, or how the crispy exterior of a chargrilled steak makes it taste meatier and more delicious. Tomatoes, soy, garlic, fish sauce, anchovies and fermented shrimp paste all create umami flavours in these sambal recipes.

Sambal is not just a condiment, but also acts as a marinade, and you will often see it used as a recipe component in this book. Nor is it limited to Asian dishes, as it can be added to almost anything that can take a little heat: try smothering sambal over crispy baked potatoes (like an Indonesian patatas bravas), mixing it with mayonnaise as a dipping sauce, or drizzling it over pizza in the way you would use a chilli oil or as a spicy relish on a hamburger. It's utterly addictive.

Tips for making sambal

- To make any sambal recipe vegan, replace the anchovies, fish sauce or fermented shrimp paste with tomato purée, soy sauce, cooked tomatoes or sun-dried tomatoes, plus a little extra salt.

- When making small quantities, using a mortar and pestle (or *cobek* and *ulekan*) will be just as quick as a food processor, but grind the hardest ingredients first to produce the best results. If you have neither a food processor nor a mortar and pestle, chop the ingredients as finely as possible.

- Do not use coconut oil when making raw or cold sambal, as it will solidify once cooled.

- Store sambal in an airtight container to retain its freshness. Most cooked sambals will keep for at least 1 week in the fridge. Where possible, cover the sambal in a thin layer of oil to preserve it.

- Most cooked sambals freeze beautifully, so cook them in larger quantities and freeze in an airtight container or ice cube trays sealed in a zip-lock bag. You can then take out only what you need. While fresh sambals are best eaten within 1 or 2 days, frozen cooked sambals will last up to 3 months.

- If your sambal is too spicy, you can diffuse the heat by cooking the sambal for longer in the pan, which will slowly mellow the spice; add something acidic to tame the heat, such as citrus juice or vinegar; add more sugar, which will counteract the spiciness; or add more ingredients or oil to dilute the chillies. Failing that, serve your sambal with lots of rice, which will help to balance the heat, and have a glass of milk on standby.

TOMATO SAMBAL
SAMBAL TOMAT

I think of this tomato relish as a beginner's guide to sambal, as it works beautifully either spicy or mild, depending on your preference. For those with chilli-sensitive palates, like my Devonshire mother-in-law, Caroline, deseeding the chillies lowers the potency of the heat. The addition of tomatoes makes it a mellow and umami-rich relish that is irresistible drizzled over soups, added to stews or used as a dipping sauce with wedges or fritters.

This is typically made with intensely flavoured bush tomatoes in the parts of Indonesia where they are lucky enough to grow them, but in my home kitchen in London I'm happy to use good-quality cherry tomatoes.

This sambal keeps for up to 1 week in the fridge covered with a thin layer of sunflower oil, or for up to 3 months in the freezer.

Origin Popular all over Indonesia
Chilli heat Moderate
Makes 250g (about 16 portions)

———

20 long red chillies (about 250g), sliced (deseeded if you prefer less heat)
2 garlic cloves, peeled and sliced
4cm piece of ginger (about 20g), peeled and sliced
2 small banana shallots or 4 Thai shallots, peeled and sliced
180g cherry tomatoes
1 tsp tamarind paste (or 1 tsp lime juice mixed with 1 tsp brown sugar)
½ tsp palm sugar or brown sugar
Sea salt and black pepper, to taste
Coconut oil or sunflower oil, for frying

———

Place the chillies, garlic, ginger, shallots and tomatoes in a food processor and blend to a semi-fine paste, retaining a little texture.

Place a frying pan over a medium heat and add 4 tablespoons of oil. Add the paste to the pan and cook, stirring continuously, for 10–15 minutes or until the sambal darkens, is fragrant and reduces to a thick consistency. Season with the tamarind paste, sugar, salt and pepper. Leave to cool.

195 Sambal

FRESH TOMATO AND BASIL DABU-DABU
DABU-DABU MANADO

This gorgeous relish hails from Manado in Sulawesi, an area famous for its love of spicy food and use of fresh herbs such as lemon basil, known as *kemangi*. *Dabu-dabu*, as they call it, holds its own as a divine, refreshing side salad that pairs beautifully with seafood, pork and chicken. Rich in citrus flavour, the juice of the tomatoes balances perfectly with the sharpness and heat of the shallots and chillies, and the addition of the lemon basil gives the dish a heavenly fragrance.

Traditionally, *dabu-dabu* is served very hot with small bird's eye chillies, but I've mellowed this version to give it extra versatility. If you want to try it the authentic way, substitute the 4 long red chillies in the recipe with 4–6 bird's eye chillies. Best eaten within 2 days.

Origin Manado, Sulawesi
Chilli heat Moderate
Makes 500g (4 portions as a side and 16 portions as a relish)

───

4 long red chillies, finely chopped (deseeded if you prefer less heat)
4 small banana shallots or 8 Thai shallots, peeled and thinly sliced
8 large tomatoes or 30 cherry tomatoes, chopped into 1cm chunks
Zest and juice of 2 limes
1½–2 tsp sea salt flakes, to taste
3 tsp palm sugar or brown sugar
Large handful of lemon basil, Thai basil or Italian basil leaves, roughly torn

───

Place the chillies, shallots, tomatoes, lime zest and juice in a bowl. Season with the salt and sugar and leave to sit for 15 minutes to allow the flavours to combine. Strain the liquid from the relish through a sieve, reserving any excess liquid as extra seasoning if you need it. Stir the basil leaves through the sambal just before serving.

197 Sambal

SOY, GARLIC AND CHILLI DIPPING SAUCE
SAMBAL KECAP ASIN

The first time I tried this sambal was one of those 'wow' moments – I had to stop myself downing it like a shot of tequila! Luckily, it has no unwelcome hangover side effects, so I fully encourage you to make it a lot. Using light soy sauce gives the sambal a salty finish, which means it can be used as a brilliant dipping sauce for dumplings and spring rolls. It's also delicious drizzled over a cold noodle salad or splashed into a wok full of stir-fried vegetables just before serving. It keeps for up to 3 days in the fridge.

Pictured with Borneo pork and prawn dumplings, p.44

Origin Popular all over Indonesia
Chilli heat Moderate
Makes About 120ml (4 portions as a dipping sauce)

——

2 small banana shallots or 4 Thai shallots, peeled and very thinly sliced
1 bird's eye chilli, deseeded and very finely chopped
2 garlic cloves, peeled and very thinly sliced
Zest of 2 limes and juice of 1–2 limes, to taste
2 tbsp light soy sauce
1 tbsp sunflower oil
Palm sugar or brown sugar, to taste
Sea salt and black pepper, to taste

——

Combine the shallots, chilli, garlic, lime zest, soy sauce and oil together in a bowl. Season with the lime juice, sugar, salt and pepper and leave to sit for 15 minutes before serving, to allow the flavours to combine.

GROUND CHILLI SAMBAL ULEK
SAMBAL ULEK

The word *ulek* is derived from *oelek*, the Dutch spelling for the Indonesian mortar and pestle that locals call *cobek* and *ulekan*. The simplest sambal to make, it calls for only chillies, vinegar and seasoning. The acid from the vinegar balances any sweeter meal, but this versatile sambal also pairs well with any dish in this book. It is an easy recipe to grind in a mortar and pestle if you have one, but it also works well in a food processor. It is the perfect sambal to rustle up when you're short of time and ingredients.

It keeps for up to 1 week in the fridge, covered with a thin layer of sunflower oil, or for up to 3 months in the freezer.

Pictured with Egg and spring onion martabak, p.39

Origin Popular all over Indonesia
Chilli heat Moderate
Makes About 120g (8 servings as a relish)

———

18 long red chillies (about 230g), half deseeded
    (or all deseeded if you prefer less heat)
1 tbsp rice vinegar or white wine vinegar
1 tbsp sunflower oil
½ tsp sugar
1 tsp sea salt
¼ tsp white pepper

———

Bring a pan of salted water to the boil. Chop the chillies into 3cm chunks and add to the salted boiling water. Return to the boil and simmer for 5 minutes before draining.

Grind the chillies with the vinegar, oil, sugar, salt and pepper in a mortar and pestle, or alternatively place all the ingredients in a small food processor and pulse to a semi-fine consistency that still has a little texture.

CARAMELISED SHALLOT SAMBAL BAWANG
SAMBAL BAWANG

This sambal is one of the simplest to make and is beautiful in appearance as well as taste. It is also one of the hottest. The coarsely ground shallots, garlic and chillies caramelise as they cook down in the fragrant oil, producing a sambal that is as delicious as it is vibrant, and it tastes incredible with anything that loves a drizzle of ketchup or chilli sauce.

This sambal keeps for up to 1 week in the fridge covered with a thin layer of sunflower oil, or for up to 3 months in the freezer.

Origin Popular all over Indonesia
Chilli heat Hot
Makes About 120g (8 portions as a relish)

———

16 long red chillies (about 200g), sliced (deseeded if you prefer less heat)
3 small banana shallots or 6 Thai shallots, peeled and sliced
5 garlic cloves, peeled and sliced
Palm sugar or brown sugar, to taste
Sea salt and ground white pepper, to taste
Coconut oil or sunflower oil, for frying

———

Heat 2 tablespoons of oil in a frying pan or wok over a medium heat. Add the chillies, shallots and garlic and fry for 5–10 minutes or until fragrant and softened, then remove from the heat. Transfer to a small food processor and pulse to a coarse texture. Return to the pan with another 2 tablespoons of oil over a medium heat. Continue to cook the sambal for a further 10 minutes or until nicely caramelised, then season with the sugar, salt and pepper before serving.

201 Sambal

PADANG GREEN CHILLI SAMBAL
SAMBAL HIJAU PADANG

The addition of fried anchovies takes this sambal to new heights. In Padang, dried, salted anchovies known as *ikan bilis* are refreshed through deep-frying and devoured in their entirety, crispy and golden. You can purchase frozen *ikan bilis* from Asian supermarkets, but tinned anchovies are an excellent alternative.

Grinding anchovies into the paste and using whole fish as a garnish is the traditional way to make and serve this versatile sambal. The resulting flavour has the right amount of saltiness balanced with the sweetness of shallots, the acidity of lime and the warmth of chilli. It is the perfect accompaniment to Beef rendang (p.166) or any rich curry that needs acidity for balance. A foodie confession: it also tastes amazing with pizza or lasagne and is great drizzled over morning eggs. I use any green chillies I have to hand, from jalapeño to serrano.

This sambal will keep for up to 1 week in the fridge in an airtight container or for up to 3 months in the freezer.

Origin Padang, Sumatra
Chilli heat Moderate
Makes About 140g (9 portions as a relish)

14 long green chillies (about 160g), halved
1 small banana shallot or 2 Thai shallots, peeled and sliced
2 garlic cloves, peeled and sliced
2 kaffir lime leaves (optional)
30g frozen ikan bilis (or 6 tinned anchovy fillets)
Juice of ½ lime
Large pinch of sea salt
Sunflower oil, for frying and deep-frying

Remove all the pith and seeds from the green chillies and reserve in a separate bowl, then finely slice the chillies. Heat 2 tablespoons of oil in a frying pan over a medium heat. Add the chillies, shallot, garlic and kaffir lime leaves, if using, and fry until softened and fragrant, about 10–15 minutes. Transfer to a bowl. Add another 1 tablespoon of oil to the pan and add the chilli seeds and pith. Cook until soft, then set aside.

Fill a deep saucepan one-third full with oil and heat it to 140°C over a high heat. (If you do not have a kitchen thermometer, use an ikan bilis to check the temperature – it should float to the surface within 1–2 seconds.) Fry the fish a handful at a time – the oil will foam and bubble – until golden. Remove the fish from the oil using a slotted spoon and drain on a tray lined with paper towels to absorb any excess oil. (If using tinned anchovies, heat 1 tablespoon of oil in a frying pan over a high heat. When the oil is shimmering, fry the anchovy fillets for 1–2 minutes, then remove from the heat.)

Remove the kaffir lime leaves from the fried chilli mixture, then place the mixture in a small food processor along with half of the reserved chilli pith and seeds and half of the fried ikan bilis or anchovies. Pulse to a coarse paste. (Alternatively, you can grind it in a pestle and mortar.) Taste and adjust the heat as necessary – for a hotter sambal, add the remaining pith and seeds. Season with the lime juice and salt.

To finish, heat 1 tablespoon of oil in the pan. Pour the hot oil over the sambal to preserve it and retain its colour.

To serve, garnish the sambal with the remaining fried ikan bilis or anchovies.

PEANUT SAUCE
SAMBAL KACANG

There are as many ways to make peanut sauce as there are sambals, but the most obvious differences are between those made with peanut butter and those made from scratch using raw peanuts fried in hot oil. I asked many Indonesians why so many of their recipes use peanut butter if the authentic way is better. 'For Westerners!' they all answered. My Australian mother loves to make a quick peanut butter satay sauce, so I do feel an affinity for the Western way, but it really is worth the extra effort to deep-fry the peanuts, as it gives a nuttier depth of flavour and a darker colour.

In Timorese communities where oil is scarce, peanuts are dry-roasted in woks filled with hot sand from the beach, the heat of the sun and sand turning the peanuts a lovely golden brown. You can also roast peanuts in the oven, which produces a result nearly as good as the fried version, but for me, deep-fried is best. However, I have provided an alternative that uses peanut butter, to tip my hat to all the home cooks out there who love a good shortcut.

Peanut sauce is great drizzled over salads, on burgers or any grilled meat, or served with satay skewers or vegetables. It will last for up to 4 days in the fridge or up to 3 months in the freezer.

Origin Popular all over Indonesia
Chilli heat Mild
Makes 150g (2 portions as a dressing or dipping sauce)

75g unsalted, raw peanuts, preferably with their skin on (or 75g unsweetened, unsalted smooth peanut butter)
2 long red chillies, deseeded and very finely chopped
1 garlic clove, peeled and crushed
4 tsp kecap manis (p.254), or more to taste
2 tsp tamarind paste (or 2 tsp lime juice mixed with 2 tsp brown sugar)
Large pinch of sea salt
Sunflower oil, for frying

If using raw peanuts, heat 150ml of oil to 160°C in a deep saucepan over a high heat. (If you do not have a kitchen thermometer, check the oil is at temperature by adding a cube of bread; it should turn golden in 25–30 seconds.) Carefully lower the peanuts into the hot oil using a slotted spoon. Stirring continuously, as peanuts can easily burn, fry for 4–5 minutes until golden. Remove the peanuts from the pan with a slotted spoon and transfer to a tray lined with paper towels to absorb any excess oil.

Heat 1 tablespoon of oil in a frying pan over a medium heat, add the chillies and garlic and fry until softened, about 4 minutes.

Place the fried peanuts or peanut butter in a small food processor with the cooked garlic and chillies, kecap manis, tamarind paste and salt. Pulse briefly, then add a splash of water to loosen the sauce and pulse again. Gradually add water (about 4 tablespoons) and continue to pulse until the sauce is a pourable consistency. Season with salt or more kecap manis as needed.

FRESH BALINESE SAMBAL MATAH
SAMBAL MATAH

Ask any Balinese native for their favourite sambal and they will tell you *sambal matah*, the raw, fresh and citrusy relish that is a dish of pride on the island of the gods. It is stirred through rice, laid upon grilled seafood, chicken, pork and satay and should be eaten just like any other sambal, a little with every mouthful. *Sambal matah* is also beautiful tossed together with leafy greens, or with a smoked fish or chicken salad. The distinctive flavour from this sambal lies in the fresh lemongrass, ginger and kaffir lime, providing a wonderful fragrance that will transport you to the tropics. If you can't find kaffir lime, use the juice and zest of a ripe lime instead. Best eaten on the day it is made.

Origin Bali
Chilli heat Moderate
Makes 140g (about 4 portions)

---

3 small banana shallots or 6 Thai shallots, peeled and thinly sliced

4cm piece of ginger (about 20g), peeled and cut into matchsticks

1 garlic clove, peeled and thinly sliced

2 long red chillies, finely chopped (deseeded if you prefer less heat)

2 lemongrass stalks, outer woody layers removed, thinly sliced

Zest and juice of 1 kaffir lime or 1 standard lime, plus extra juice to taste

2 kaffir lime leaves, stems removed, thinly sliced (or the zest and juice of 1 standard lime)

Palm sugar or brown sugar, to taste

Sea salt, to taste

Sunflower oil, for drizzling

Place the sliced shallots in a bowl and sprinkle with a generous pinch of salt. Set aside for at least 15 minutes. This will take the raw edge off them.

Mix together the ginger, garlic, chillies, lemongrass, lime zest and juice and kaffir lime leaves. Add the shallots and season the sambal with sugar, salt and additional lime juice, to taste. Drizzle with the oil and serve.

207 Sambal

FERMENTED SHRIMP SAMBAL TERASI
SAMBAL TERASI KUPANG

I've seen many variations of *sambal terasi* all over Indonesia and everyone's mother seems to have her own recipe. This version was taught to me by my aunty Tje Ie in her blue-tiled kitchen in Kupang, Timor, and is my favourite version. I love the drizzle of fish sauce to finish, giving it the ultimate punch in tandem with the lime. If you can't get your hands on Indonesian shrimp paste, *terasi*, substitute with Thai shrimp paste or more fish sauce, adding a little at a time until you hit the umami flavour note.

This sambal pairs perfectly with fish and seafood dishes and lasts for 1 week in the fridge under a thin layer of sunflower oil, and 3 months in the freezer.

Pictured with Medanese prawn bisque, p.63

Origin Kupang, Timor
Chilli heat Hot
Makes About 100g (6 portions as a relish)

———

20 long red chillies (about 240g), half deseeded, all sliced
1 tsp Roasted fermented shrimp paste (p.253), or Thai shrimp paste or 2 tsp good-quality fish sauce
2 tbsp coconut oil or sunflower oil
Large pinch of salt
Juice of 2 limes
Good-quality fish sauce, to taste

———

Place the chillies in a food processor and blend to a coarse texture, then stir together with the roasted terasi or fish sauce.

Heat the oil in a frying pan over a medium heat, add the salt and the chilli mixture and fry until fragrant, about 10–15 minutes. Season with salt, lime juice and a drizzle of fish sauce, to taste.

SULAWESI RICA-RICA CHILLI SAUCE
RICA-RICA SULAWESI

Under the shadow of Mount Mahawu, the fertile volcano in North Sulawesi, I learnt to make *rica-rica*. A name that literally translates as 'chilli-chilli' in the Sulawesi dialect, this is a sauce known to set the mouth on fire. The letter 'c' in the word *rica* is pronounced 'ch' in Bahasa Indonesian, as in 'chilli'. Here it is eaten with nearly every local dish, including fragrant lemon basil stir-fries, as a dipping sauce with satays and as a marinade for grilled meats.

In the interests of self-preservation, I deseed half the chillies for this recipe. If you want to eat like the Sulawesi do, keep all the pith and seeds to see how high your chilli tolerance goes. *Rica-rica* lasts for a week in the fridge under a thin layer of sunflower oil, and 3 months in the freezer.

Pictured with Egg crepe rolls, p.157

Origin Manado, Sulawesi
Chilli heat Hot
Makes About 160g (10 portions as a relish)

———

16 long red chillies (about 200g), half deseeded, all sliced
4 garlic cloves, peeled and sliced
4 small banana shallots or 8 Thai shallots, peeled and sliced
4cm piece of ginger (about 20g), peeled and sliced
2 tbsp coconut oil or sunflower oil
Lime juice, to taste
Palm sugar or brown sugar, to taste
Sea salt, to taste

———

Place the chillies, garlic, shallots and ginger in a food processor and blend to a smooth paste. Heat the oil in a frying pan over a medium heat. Add the spice paste and fry, stirring continuously, until fragrant, about 10–15 minutes. Remove from the heat and transfer to a bowl. Season with lime juice, sugar and salt to taste until the sambal is well-balanced and delicious.

SWEETS

—

The Indonesian approach to sweet food is very different to that of the West. You will often be presented with an exquisite plate of tropical fruits to finish a meal, but desserts as we understand them don't exist. In the same way Westerners enjoy an afternoon biscuit, you will find bite-sized Indonesian sweets offered as a welcome snack when visiting a home, often placed on a saucer with your cup of coffee or tea. Known as *jajanan pasar* (which translates as 'market snacks'), these sweets boast over one thousand years of history and date back to the ninth century, when recognisable cakes were found inscribed on the sides of Prambanan temple in central Java.

Entire *jajanan pasar* food markets, like the Pasar Kue Subuh in south Jakarta, are dedicated to these rainbow-coloured sweet snacks, which are enjoyed by Indonesians at all times of day. More than 50 merchants lay thousands of their sweets side by side in large cardboard and plastic trays, an assortment of cakes, biscuits and breads stained in fluorescent shades of green, pink, yellow and red, some shaped using intricate patterned moulds and others simply wrapped in banana leaves. Trading begins at 4.00 a.m. and less than three hours later most have sold out, such is the enthusiasm of locals and tourists who wish to secure their daily supply. Each snack is small, enough for only a bite or two, and rice and tapioca flour, palm sugar and coconut form the base of most recipes. My favourites include the pandan-flavoured *klepon* (p.224), a green glutinous rice ball dusted in grated coconut and filled with melted palm sugar that bursts in the mouth with a single bite, and is best eaten with a cup of hot coffee in the morning. Then there is Indonesia's answer to the doughnut, *kue perut ayam* (p.218), coiled into a spiral shape with soft, fluffy insides and crispy exterior.

Sweet street-food snacks are as popular as their savoury counterparts in Indonesia. I became accustomed to buying freshly fried banana fritters, known as *pisang goreng* (p.222), from the passing mobile carts that I found in every major city. Eaten off nothing more than a paper napkin – the crispy batter infused with sticky palm sugar a stark contrast to the warm, ripe bananas inside – every bite was luxurious. Likewise, I found *kue lapis legit*, or thousand-layer cake (p.240), in every market I visited. A richly layered cake with notes of cinnamon, ginger, cardamom and nutmeg, it is a nationally loved sweet treat that makes an appearance at almost every special occasion across the country.

In the interest of my own love of desserts, I've included a few recipes in this chapter that are not authentic Indonesian sweets but are inspired by the flavours of the region. My pandan and coconut cake (p.238) is an adaptation of a steamed pudding that my grandmother Popo used to make for me when I was little. My version uses a fluffy sponge that is lightly textured from the desiccated coconut and coconut milk used in the batter, with a mascarpone and raspberry or lemon filling. Coconut-inspired desserts such as my coconut panna cotta (p.230) or coconut and lime ice cream (p.227) are a light and refreshing way to finish an Indonesian meal, and incredibly easy to put together in less than 30 minutes. For chocolate lovers, my chilli chocolate and salted nut caramel tart (p.232) is a heavenly and decadent dessert worthy of a second serving. Fresh ginger is the star of my sticky ginger toffee pudding (p.236), served with a butterscotch sauce that is spiked with the heat of chilli and the crunch of macadamias, a dessert that can be made in advance and frozen for those who like to prepare ahead of time.

This chapter is dedicated to my grandmother Popo, whose sweet recipes have found a new home in my London kitchen. It includes the recipes that I discovered in her notebooks as well as those passed down from her to my aunties, and then to me in turn. There are also many traditional recipes I learnt from home cooks across the archipelago, who say that when we eat *jajanan pasar* we are eating the wisdom of our ancestors: one thousand years of history. Created as a symbol of Indonesia's diversity and the great wave of ethnicities, personalities and struggles that found a home on these islands, *jajanan pasar* serve as a reminder to Indonesians to be tolerant and kind to each other. I hope that eating and sharing the sweets from this selection of recipes and stories can do exactly that for us.

PANDAN CREPES
DADAR GULUNG

I have eaten *dadar gulung* for breakfast many times in Indonesia. The pancake is a vibrant green, tinted from the juice of pandan, a plant that grows all over Indonesia and lends a herby, grassy aroma to food. The mixture of sweetened grated coconut with the slightly savoury pandan makes these fragrant pancakes irresistible. Be sure to finely slice the pandan leaves before blending them – you need to shred the leaves to a very fine pulp to extract as much juice and colour as possible. (You can find pandan extract but I prefer not to use it as I find the taste too artificial.)

You can eat this for breakfast or as a Western-style dessert. Indonesians also like to fill the pancake with ripe jackfruit, so you could do that too, or use bananas, mangoes and other tropical fruits to add another dimension. You will need a small, non-stick frying pan for this recipe – I use a 20cm pan.

Origin Popular all over Indonesia
Makes 16

12 pandan leaves, very thinly sliced (or ½ tsp vanilla extract and an optional drop of green food colouring)
150g plain flour
Pinch of sea salt
2 medium eggs
150ml coconut milk
150g unsweetened desiccated coconut
150g palm sugar or brown sugar
Coconut oil or sunflower oil, for frying

Place the shredded pandan leaves in a food processor with 200ml water and blend to a fine pulp. Push the pulp and any juice through a sieve. You need 165ml of liquid, so if you do not have enough, top up with more water and blend again. If you're not using pandan leaves, mix the vanilla extract and optional green food colouring with 165ml water.

Sift the flour into a mixing bowl and add the salt. Crack the eggs into a jug and mix with the coconut milk and pandan juice or vanilla water. Make a well in the flour and gradually add the coconut mixture, whisking vigorously in between additions to remove any lumps. The batter should have a smooth consistency. If you find any lumps, pass the batter through a sieve. Let the batter rest for a minimum of 1 hour in the fridge.

To make the filling, place the desiccated coconut and palm sugar in a pan over a medium heat with 100ml water. Boil the mixture until there is no liquid left in the pan, stirring continuously – this will take about 5 minutes. Set aside to cool.

Add 1 teaspoon of oil to a small non-stick frying pan, then wipe it around with a paper towel. Heat the pan over a medium-low heat. Once hot, pour 2 tablespoons of batter into the pan and swirl it around to create a very thin layer, ensuring there is even coverage. Pour away any excess. Use a teaspoon to smooth the batter, if needed, and add extra batter to fill any holes. Cook the pancake for 15 seconds on each side. Transfer to a plate using a spatula.

To fill the pancakes, place a pancake on a chopping board and spoon about a tablespoon of the filling on the bottom half. Fold the left and right sides over first, and then roll the pancake up into a cigar shape. Cut each pancake in half on the diagonal before serving.

INDONESIAN CINNAMON DOUGHNUTS
KUE PERUT AYAM

My aunty Tje Ie taught me how to make *kue perut ayam*, a coiled fluffy doughnut dusted in cinnamon sugar. The name translates as 'chicken stomach cake', but happily this sweet tastes more appetising than that name suggests. A famed sweet in the Timorese town of Kupang, the batter is piped in a long, thin coil resembling a chicken's intestine. Legend states that a son can only gain his parents' permission to marry a girl if she can make a *kue perut ayam* that is perfect in texture, shape and flavour. If she fails, they are forbidden to marry. Luckily for my husband Nick, I got the hang of it after a couple of tries.

You can determine your future destiny in love with this recipe, but don't worry – even failed attempts taste divine. As well as needing a piping bag, you must cook these doughnuts in a wok, because the bowl shape of the wok keeps the coil intact. (A standard frying pan will not do, as the doughnuts will spread to the width of the pan.)

Origin Kupang, Timor
Makes 12

————

150g caster sugar
2 tsp ground cinnamon
Sunflower oil, for frying

For the batter
300g plain flour
1 tsp bicarbonate of soda
Large pinch of sea salt
150g caster sugar
4 medium eggs
2 tsp vanilla extract
2 tbsp unsalted butter, melted

————

To make the batter, sift the flour, bicarbonate of soda and salt into a large bowl and stir together with the sugar. Whisk the eggs, vanilla extract and melted butter with 4 tablespoons of water in a jug. Make a well in the flour and gradually add the egg mixture, whisking vigorously in between additions to remove any lumps. Let the batter rest for a minimum of 1 hour in the fridge. Remove the batter from the fridge 30 minutes before cooking to allow it to come to room temperature.

Combine the sugar and cinnamon in a bowl and set aside.

Fill a wok with oil to a depth of 1cm. Heat the oil to 160ºC. (If you do not have a kitchen thermometer, check the oil is at temperature by adding a cube of bread; it should turn golden in 25–30 seconds.) It is important the oil stays at 160ºC, otherwise the doughnuts will undercook or burn and dry out.

Fill a piping bag with the batter and massage the bag briefly with your hands to warm it. Cut an

Continues overleaf

opening about 1cm wide at the tip. While piping, keep an even speed and pressure throughout and work in a continual motion. Starting in the centre of the wok with the tip of the piping bag close to the oil, carefully squeeze the bag until the batter drops into the hot oil and then, moving outwards in a spiral shape, swiftly coil the batter around the centre three times. The rings of the coil must not touch each other as they hit the oil because the dough puffs up as it cooks. After the third loop, stop squeezing and let the tail of the batter fall back over the coils to fix the doughnut in its circular shape.

After 2–3 minutes, the doughnut will have bubbled on the surface and be light golden underneath. Using a fish slice or spatula, flip it over to cook on the other side for a further 2–3 minutes. This is the presentation side, which will be a perfect coil when flipped over. Once cooked, transfer to a tray lined with paper towels to absorb any excess oil. Check the dough is not raw in the centre – if so, adjust the cooking time and oil temperature accordingly.

Repeat until all the batter has been used. It takes practice to get the hang of piping the doughnuts, so consider your first attempt as a practice run.

Toss the doughnuts in the bowl of cinnamon sugar. Serve immediately.

BANANA FRITTERS
PISANG GORENG

Street-food vendors will typically put their own spin on *pisang goreng*, the deep-fried banana and plantain fritters famous all over Indonesia. Most batter and fry the bananas whole, others cut the fruit into the shape of a fan, while the rest thinly slice the bananas to produce a round fritter thick with batter. In West Jakarta, Ibu Nanik's version has locals lining up to buy boxes of twenty honey-laden *pisang goreng* at a time. Her fritters are dark and caramelised, with a crispy exterior and a soft, cake-like interior. It's easy to see why you might want to buy more than one.

This is my version of Ibu Nanik's honeyed banana fritters. Choosing only ripe bananas for this dish adds a natural sweetness and creaminess that is unbelievably moreish. The fritters are best served immediately, but if you have any left over, you can reheat them in the oven at 170°C/150°C fan/gas 3 for 10 minutes. Enjoy on their own or, if you're feeling extra indulgent, serve with a side of vanilla ice cream or clotted cream.

Origin Popular all over Indonesia
Makes About 12

150g plain flour
65g rice flour
2 tsp cornflour
1 tsp baking powder
½ tsp sea salt
80ml coconut milk
2 tbsp melted butter
½ tsp vanilla extract
3½ tbsp good-quality runny honey
1 tbsp palm sugar or brown sugar
6 ripe bananas, cut into thin, round slices
Sunflower oil, for deep-frying

Sift the plain flour, rice flour and cornflour into a large mixing bowl and add the baking powder and salt. Mix the coconut milk, melted butter, vanilla extract, honey, sugar and 130ml water together in a jug. Make a well in the flour and gradually add the coconut mixture, whisking vigorously in between additions to remove any lumps. Let the batter rest for 15 minutes in the fridge.

After the batter has rested, add the sliced bananas to the bowl and stir through the mix.

Fill a deep non-stick saucepan or large wok one-third full with oil. Heat the oil to 180°C. (If you do not have a kitchen thermometer, check the oil is at temperature by adding a cube of bread; it should turn golden in 15 seconds.)

Using a large serving spoon, scoop up some of the batter and bananas, then carefully pour it into the hot oil – the fritter will look a little rustic but that's part of its charm. Repeat until you have made 6–8 fritters, without overcrowding the pan. Fry the fritters for 2–3 minutes on each side or until crisp, caramelised and a deep golden colour. During cooking, gently lift up each fritter as it cooks using a palette knife or metal spatula. If you are not using a non-stick pan, the fritters may stick to the base of the pan.

Remove from the pan with tongs or a slotted spoon and place on a tray lined with paper towels to absorb any excess oil, without overlapping them, so they don't go soggy.

Repeat until all the batter is used, topping up the oil if necessary. Serve immediately.

COCONUT STICKY RICE BALLS
KLEPON

Indonesian sweets often feature an element of surprise. When I first tried the chewy glutinous rice balls called *klepon,* I was amazed by their liquid palm sugar centres that burst like soup dumplings as soon as you take a bite. It's common to be served these little treats with coffee in the morning, or at any one of the many snack points that mark a typical Indonesian day. The dough is usually flavoured with pandan leaves, which imparts a floral, grassy flavour in the same way we would use vanilla in the West. Be sure to finely slice your pandan leaves before blending them – you want the leaves to be shredded to a very fine pulp to extract as much juice and colour as possible. If you can't find pandan leaves, you can add a half teaspoon of vanilla extract, giving it a snowy white appearance. (You can find pandan extract but I prefer not to use it as I find the taste too artificial.) Dark palm sugar that can be grated works best for this recipe, giving a luscious caramel flavour and appearance, but the variety of palm sugar available in a jar will also do. You can find it, along with glutinous rice flour, in most Asian supermarkets.

Originating in Java, *klepon* have crossed oceans and become popular in Singapore and Malaysia where they are known as *ondeh-ondeh.* But it is Indonesia where *klepon* are still most adored, their popularity immortalised in a folk song about their wonders called *Jaja Klepon. Klepon* will last for 2 days in an airtight container at room temperature.

Origin Java
Makes 24

——

80g palm sugar or dark brown sugar
12 pandan leaves, very thinly sliced (or ½ tsp vanilla extract)
260g glutinous rice flour
120g unsweetened desiccated coconut

——

Prepare the filling by grating the palm sugar and then rolling it into 24 balls measuring 7.5mm in diameter. If using palm sugar from a jar, scoop heaped ½ teaspoons of the sugar into balls weighing about 3g each. If using brown sugar, mix it in a bowl with 1½ teaspoons of water, stir until combined and then portion into balls. If the balls are too big, you risk the sugar not completely melting inside the rice ball.

Place the pandan leaves in a food processor with 250ml water and blend to a fine pulp. Push the pulp and any juice through a sieve. You need 210ml, so top up with water if necessary and blend again. If you're not using pandan leaves, mix the vanilla extract with 210ml water.

Place the glutinous rice flour in a mixing bowl and add the 210ml pandan juice or vanilla water. Work the mixture with your hands for at least 5 minutes to make a soft dough with no streaks. You are looking for the consistency of bread dough. It should feel neither dry nor overly wet, so add some extra water or flour if needed. Cover with a clean tea towel so the dough does not dry out, then rest for 15 minutes.

Take a heaped tablespoon (about 20g) of the dough and roll a test ball. Using the tip of your

Continues overleaf

thumb, make an indentation in the ball. If the dough is pliable and does not fall apart, the dough is ready to use. If it is cracking too much or feels too thin, adjust with more water or flour as needed.

Once you are happy with the consistency, roll the dough into bite-sized balls and cover them again with the clean tea towel. It's important to ensure the balls are on the small side as, if the dough is too thick, they will be too chewy.

Make a deep thumb indentation in the middle of each dough ball and place the rolled palm sugar ball inside. Mould the dough around the palm sugar, pinching it closed to seal and roll it back into a smooth ball. Keep everything covered with the tea towel until all the balls are rolled.

Place the desiccated coconut in a bowl. Bring a saucepan filled with water to the boil over a high heat and, drop in the klepon balls in batches of 6–8 at a time. Shake the pan a little so the balls do not stick to the base. Return the water to the boil and then reduce to a rolling simmer. The klepon are cooked when they float to the surface. Remove the klepon with a slotted spoon and then toss them in the bowl of desiccated coconut. Repeat with the remaining balls, leave to cool for 5 minutes, then serve.

COCONUT AND LIME ICE CREAM
ES KRIM KELAPA DAN JERUK NIPIS

Coconut and lime are two flavours with a magical ability to transport me to the tropics, and this refreshing ice cream is no exception. Condensed milk is the secret to this ice cream, resulting in a luxuriously smooth finish that is creamy rather than icy. Toasted coconut stirred through the mixture before freezing adds the slightest crunch, and along with a hint of lime makes this light and cooling dessert the perfect finish to a meal. The mixture can be made in under 30 minutes and there is no need to churn it or mix it once it hits the freezer. It will be ready to eat in 4–6 hours and will last in the freezer for 3 months.

Makes 1.8l

——

Finely grated zest and juice (about 150ml)
    of 5 limes
20g caster sugar
100g unsweetened desiccated coconut
600ml double cream
400ml coconut milk
800ml condensed milk
Lime zest, to serve

——

Place the lime zest and juice in a saucepan with the sugar. Warm gently until the sugar dissolves, then bring to the boil. Reduce the heat and simmer until the lime juice turns syrupy. Pour the lime syrup through a heatproof sieve into a bowl. Leave to cool.

Tip the desiccated coconut into a dry frying pan over a medium heat. Shake the pan continuously until the coconut is toasted and golden. Remove from the heat and leave to cool.

Whisk the double cream to stiff peaks in a large bowl. Mix the coconut milk with the condensed milk and cooled lime syrup in another bowl. Add the condensed milk mixture to the whipped cream and whisk together until well combined. Stir through the toasted coconut.

Pour the ice-cream mixture into an airtight container. (You many need to divide the mixture between two containers.) Freeze for a minimum of 4–6 hours, but ideally overnight. Remove the container from the freezer 10 minutes before serving to allow the ice cream to soften. Serve with an extra grating of fine lime zest over every scoop.

PEANUT AND BANANA ICE CREAM
ES KRIM PISANG DAN KACANG

This soft and velvety-smooth ice cream is the perfect finish to an Indonesian meal. Homemade ice cream can be a lot of work, but this no-churn version takes only 30 minutes of hands-on time and tastes absolutely delicious. Chopped, roasted peanuts are stirred through the ice cream before freezing, giving it a lovely, crunchy texture. Once in the freezer, there is no need to do anything further and it is ready to eat in 4–6 hours.

You won't find this recipe in the traditional food markets, but it comes with all the flavours of Indonesia. If you're feeling decadent, stir dark chocolate chunks through the ice cream with the peanuts before freezing. It will keep in the freezer for 3 months.

Makes 1.6l

—

300g unsalted roasted peanuts, or 100g unsalted roasted peanuts and 200g chunky peanut butter, plus extra chopped roasted peanuts to serve
480ml double cream
400g frozen banana chunks
400ml condensed milk
80g caster sugar

—

Place 200g of the peanuts in a food processor and blend to a coarse paste. (You can skip this step if you are using peanut butter.) Roughly chop the remaining 100g peanuts and set aside.

Whisk the double cream to stiff peaks in a large bowl and set aside.

Place the frozen banana chunks in a food processor and blend until smooth. Add the condensed milk, sugar and coarse peanut paste or peanut butter and blend again.

Add the banana mixture to the whipped cream and whisk together until well combined. Stir through the reserved chopped peanuts.

Pour the ice-cream mixture into an airtight container. (You many need to divide the mixture between two containers.) Freeze for a minimum of 4–6 hours, but ideally overnight. Remove the container from the freezer 10 minutes before serving to allow the ice cream to soften. Serve sprinkled with chopped peanuts.

COCONUT PANNA COTTA WITH MANGO
PANNA COTTA KELAPA, DENGAN MANGGA

Although not traditionally an Indonesian dessert, this coconut panna cotta is inspired by all the flavours of the archipelago. The lemongrass sugar syrup and chopped mango are the perfect accompaniment for this light, creamy dessert with just the right amount of wobble. You can use any tropical fruits you like in place of the mango, such as lychees, dragonfruit, rock melon or pineapple.

This is a soft-set panna cotta that will melt in the mouth and de-mould to perfection, but exact liquid measurements must be followed. You will need six 175ml dariole moulds or mini pudding basins. The desserts will keep in the fridge for 2 days.

Serves 6

———

1 mango, peeled, stoned and cut into small cubes
Coconut oil, for greasing

For the panna cotta
500ml double cream
400ml coconut milk
80g caster sugar
1 vanilla pod, split in half and seeds scraped (or 1 tsp vanilla paste)
Pinch of sea salt
4 sheets platinum-grade leaf gelatine

For the syrup
80g caster sugar
6cm piece of ginger (about 30g), peeled and grated
2 lemongrass stalks, outer woody layers removed, very thinly sliced

To make the panna cotta, pour the double cream and coconut milk into a saucepan, then add the sugar, vanilla (including the empty pod, if using) and salt. Bring to a gentle simmer, then remove the pan from the heat. Leave to infuse for 10 minutes.

Place the gelatine leaves in a bowl and cover with cold water, then add couple of ice cubes. Leave to soak for 5 to 10 minutes, but no longer than that or the gelatine will lose its strength.

Strain the cream mixture through a sieve and return to the saucepan over a gentle heat. Remove the gelatine leaves from the bowl and squeeze out any excess water. Remove the saucepan from the heat, immediately add the gelatine to the warmed cream mixture and stir until dissolved. Strain the mixture through a sieve into a jug. Very lightly grease the dariole moulds or mini pudding basins with coconut oil, pour in the panna cotta mixture, then cover with cling film. Chill in the fridge for a minimum of 6 hours, but ideally overnight.

To make the syrup, place the sugar, ginger and lemongrass in a small saucepan and add 90ml cold water. Gently warm over a low heat until the sugar has dissolved, about 5 minutes. Bring to the boil, then reduce the heat and simmer for 10 minutes or until the liquid is thick and syrupy. Remove the pan from the heat and leave the syrup to cool. Strain the syrup through a heatproof sieve to remove and discard the lemongrass and ginger.

Remove the panna cottas from the fridge 5–10 minutes before serving. Carefully run the tip of a small knife around the edge of each mould to loosen them. You only need to insert the knife a couple of millimetres deep. Dip each mould into hot water for 10 seconds to loosen the panna cotta, then invert it onto a plate and, holding both the mould and plate tightly, give the panna cotta one firm shake sideways while still inside the mould. It should come loose. Place a couple of spoonfuls of the chopped mango beside the panna cotta and drizzle with the lemongrass syrup.

——

Variation: Vegan coconut panna cotta

If you would like to make this recipe vegan, set your panna cottas in serving glasses, as they do not de-mould easily. Replace the double cream with coconut milk and instead of gelatine, add 2.25g agar agar flakes to the warmed coconut milk. Bring it to the boil and simmer for 4 minutes to dissolve the flakes. Strain the mixture through a sieve into a jug and immediately pour it into your serving glasses, as the agar agar begins to set at 40°C. Chill before serving.

CHILLI CHOCOLATE AND NUT CARAMEL TART
KUE COKELAT DAN KACANG KARAMEL

This decadent Indonesian-inspired chocolate tart brings the subtle heat of chilli together with the roasted flavour of salted nut caramel to form an incredible dessert that is simple to make and beautifully rich. Garnish with a crumble of finely chopped nuts and a dollop of crème fraîche or cream. You will need a 23cm tart tin. The tart will keep in the fridge for 5 days.

Serves 8–12

---

2 long red chillies, finely chopped
½ tsp chilli flakes
200ml double cream
Unsalted butter, for greasing
375g ready-made all-butter shortcrust pastry
175g dark chocolate (70% cocoa), chopped into
   small pieces
Handful of unsalted roasted nuts, such as peanuts,
   hazelnuts or macadamias, roughly chopped,
   to garnish

For the salted nut caramel
50g unsalted roasted nuts, such as peanuts,
   hazelnuts or macadamias, roughly chopped
300g caster sugar
300ml double cream
75g unsalted butter
¾ tsp sea salt flakes

Place the chopped chillies, chilli flakes and cream in a saucepan and bring to a gentle boil. Remove from the heat and allow the chilli to infuse the cream for a minimum of 1 hour.

If roasting your own nuts, follow the instructions on p.106. Leave to cool, then roughly chop them.

To make the salted nut caramel, tip the sugar into a saucepan, pour in 100ml cold water and heat gently until the sugar has dissolved. Bring to the boil over a high heat and simmer for 10–12 minutes until it is a deep caramel colour – swirl it around without stirring to ensure it cooks evenly. Don't be tempted to remove it from the heat too soon, or it will be too pale.

Continues overleaf

While the caramel is boiling, place the 300ml double cream and unsalted butter in another saucepan and warm over a medium heat, ensuring the butter has melted, then set aside.

When the caramel is ready, remove the pan from the heat and immediately add the cream and butter mixture, whisking vigorously until combined. Return the pan to the hob over a medium heat and simmer for 8–10 minutes. Stir through the chopped nuts and salt, then leave to cool. Don't store the caramel in the fridge as it will harden (although it can be easily softened again by reheating).

Lightly grease a 23cm tart tin. Roll out the pastry to a thickness of 3mm and use it to line the tart tin. Trim any excess pastry from the edge with a knife and prick the base all over with a fork. Chill in the fridge for a minimum of 30 minutes before baking.

Preheat the oven to 200°C/180°C fan/gas 6. When ready to bake, cover the pastry case with baking parchment and fill with dried baking beans. Blind bake the pastry case on the top shelf of the hot oven for 10–15 minutes. Carefully remove the baking beans and parchment, then bake again for 15 minutes, or until golden. Allow to cool.

To make the chocolate ganache, strain the infused cream into a heatproof bowl and add the dark chocolate pieces. Place a little water in a small saucepan and place over a low heat. Rest the heatproof bowl on top of the saucepan and stir the chocolate and cream together until the chocolate is entirely melted.

Spoon generous amounts of the caramel into the pastry case to cover the base. Pour over the chocolate ganache, cover with cling film and chill in the fridge until completely cool. When ready to serve, scatter over the extra chopped nuts and cut into slices.

PALM SUGAR SLICE
KUE GULA MERAH

Mouthwatering flavours of caramel and molasses ooze over a sweet palm sugar crumble base in this modern interpretation of Indonesian brown sugar cake. Served warm with a centre that is gooey, decadent and delicious, this traybake has all the flavours and textures that I adore.

I bake it in a 20cm square tin and then cut each slice to the size of a brownie. It can be pre-sliced and then frozen for up to 3 months in an airtight container. When eaten fresh, the slices last for 3 days in the fridge, and they are incredible when reheated for 30 seconds in the microwave or for 5–8 minutes at 170°C/150°C fan/gas 3 in the oven.

Put the leftover egg whites to good use by making meringues or a pavlova, or egg white omelettes for breakfast. Egg whites can also be frozen for up to a year, and for ease of access you can freeze them individually in ice cube trays, covered and sealed.

——

Makes 20 slices

——

For the crumble
300g unsalted butter, softened
300g palm sugar or brown sugar
450g plain flour, sifted

For the cake
75g ground almonds
100g caster sugar
200g palm sugar or brown sugar
Large pinch of sea salt
50g milk powder (optional)
150g unsalted butter, melted
200ml double cream
8 medium egg yolks

Preheat the oven to 180°C/160°C fan/gas 4. Line a 20cm square cake tin with baking parchment.

To make the crumble, beat the butter and sugar together with an electric whisk until pale and fluffy. Add the flour and stir together until well combined. Set aside.

To make the cake, combine the almonds, sugars, salt and milk powder, if using, in a bowl. Add the melted butter and mix with a wooden spoon. Add the cream, mixing together again and finally add the yolks, stirring everything until well combined.

Pat the crumble into the base of the lined cake tin, making sure it is no thicker than 5mm. Pour the cake mix over the crumble base, spreading it out into an even layer.

Bake on the middle shelf for 45–55 minutes or until a skewer inserted in the centre comes out with some moist crumbs clinging to it. Allow to cool completely in the tin before slicing, otherwise the cake will crumble. However, if you don't mind a little bit of gooey mess, you can cut it while still warm from the oven.

STICKY GINGER TOFFEE PUDDING
KUE JAHE DAN KARAMEL

Fresh ginger is the star in these divine sticky ginger toffee puddings, giving the dessert a refreshing fiery kick. This rich toffee dessert is warmed by the heat of chilli and enlivened by the crunch of macadamias in the butterscotch sauce, and can be served with cream, ice cream or whipped coconut cream.

The puddings can be made ahead of time if you like, lasting up to 5 days in the fridge or 3 months in the freezer. Defrost at room temperature and then reheat in a low oven at 140°C/120°C fan/gas 1, covered in foil, for 15 minutes before serving. You will need eight 175ml dariole moulds or mini pudding basins.

——

Serves 8

——

225g unsalted butter, softened, plus 2 tbsp
120ml whole milk
100g pitted medjool dates, diced
230g light brown sugar
7cm piece of ginger (about 35g), peeled and
    finely grated
2 medium eggs
1½ tbsp golden syrup
225g self-raising flour, sifted
Cream, whipped coconut cream or ice cream,
    to serve
Handful of macadamia nuts, roughly chopped,
    to serve

For the butterscotch sauce
50g macadamia nuts
100g light brown sugar
125ml double cream
25g unsalted butter
½ tsp sea salt
1 tsp chilli flakes (optional)

Melt the 2 tablespoons of butter, use some to brush the inside of the moulds, then chill them in the fridge. Once it has hardened, brush on another layer of butter and return to the fridge. Line the bases with circles of baking parchment and place the moulds on a baking tray.

Preheat the oven to 190°C/170°C fan/gas 5. Scatter the macadamia nuts over a baking tray and bake in the hot oven for 12–15 minutes or until golden. Set aside to cool and then roughly chop. Reduce the oven temperature to 180°C/160°C fan/gas 4.

Pour the milk into a small saucepan with the dates and bring to the boil. Remove from the heat and leave to infuse for 30 minutes.

Beat the 225g butter with the sugar and fresh ginger in a large mixing bowl until pale and fluffy, about 3–5 minutes. Add the eggs one at a time, beating in between additions, then stir in the golden syrup. Fold in the milk and dates, then fold in the flour until just combined.

Divide the mixture between the moulds, no more than two-thirds full. Bake on the middle shelf of the oven for 22–25 minutes or until a skewer poked into the centre comes out clean.

Meanwhile, to make the butterscotch sauce, combine the sugar, cream and butter in a pan over a low heat and warm until the sugar has dissolved and the butter has melted. Bring to the boil, then reduce to a simmer for 5 minutes. Stir through the macadamias, salt and chilli flakes, if using.

Wearing oven gloves as the moulds will be hot, carefully loosen the puddings by running the tip of a small knife around the edges of the moulds. Invert each pudding onto a plate and pour over the warm butterscotch sauce. Serve with cream or ice cream and a sprinkling of extra macadamias.

PANDAN AND COCONUT CAKE
KUE PANDAN DAN KELAPA

This sponge is inspired by a cake my grandmother Popo used to make. I have many happy memories of watching her lovingly prepare it, a ritual that always ended with me licking the green batter from the spoon and bowl. The desiccated coconut and coconut milk in the recipe gives the fluffy sponge its light crumb and texture. The juice from the pandan leaves gives the cake a luminous leaf-green colour (if you can't get hold of pandan leaves, try my equally delicious raspberry variation below). Finely chopping the pandan leaves ensures that you extract maximum juice and colour. I avoid pandan pastes and extracts as they taste too artificial.

––––––

Serves 16

––––––

12 pandan leaves, very thinly sliced
210ml coconut milk
70g unsweetened desiccated coconut
350g unsalted butter, softened, plus extra
   for greasing
420g caster sugar
4 medium eggs, at room temperature
385g plain flour
3½ tsp baking powder
Pinch of sea salt

For the filling
250g mascarpone cheese
75g shop-bought lemon curd or raspberry jam

To finish
2 tbsp unsweetened desiccated coconut
Icing sugar

––––––

Preheat the oven to 180°C/160°C fan/gas 4. Grease 2 x 20cm round, deep cake tins, then line with baking parchment on the base and sides.

Put the sliced pandan leaves in a food processor with 100ml water and blend to a fine pulp. Push the pulp and juice through a sieve. You need 75ml of liquid, so blend the pulp with more water if you do not have enough.

Pour the coconut milk into a saucepan and heat gently until steam rises. Remove from the heat, add the desiccated coconut and pandan juice and set aside to let the flavours infuse.

Beat the butter and caster sugar in a mixing bowl until pale and creamy, about 3–4 minutes. Add the eggs one at a time, beating between each addition. Add the coconut and pandan mixture to the butter, sugar and eggs and combine.

Sift the flour, baking powder and salt into a separate bowl. Add the dry ingredients to the cake mixture and fold in quickly until the mixture is no longer streaky. Divide the mixture between the cake tins and smooth the tops. Bake on the middle shelf for 35–45 minutes or until a skewer comes out clean. Allow to cool for 5 minutes in the tin, then turn out onto a wire rack to cool.

For the filling, beat the mascarpone cheese in a bowl to loosen it, then very lightly stir through the lemon curd or raspberry jam to create swirls. Sandwich the cake halves together with the mascarpone filling. Toast the desiccated coconut for the garnish in a dry frying pan over a medium heat until golden brown. To finish, dust the top of the cake with icing sugar and scatter over the toasted coconut.

––––––

Variation: Raspberry and coconut cake

Replace the pandan with 1½ tsp vanilla extract. At the end of mixing the batter, stir through 210g fresh raspberries and cook as above.

THOUSAND-LAYER CAKE
KUE LAPIS LEGIT

Kue lapis legit is one of the most celebrated cakes in Indonesia: a spiced, buttery sponge made of thin golden layers rich in cinnamon, nutmeg, ginger and cardamom. The cake uses an unconventional cooking method, as each layer is grilled individually for a couple of minutes. By no means does this make it dry – with 22 egg yolks and a high butter content, the cake is rich and moist and lasts for at least a week in the fridge. (For ideas for using up leftover egg whites, see the recipe introduction on p.235.)

The traditional *kue lapis legit* made by my grandmother Popo boasted more than 18 layers and could serve up to 40 people (no more than a small slice was needed when the cake was so rich). It goes by different names: *spekkoek* or 'bacon cake' in Dutch, due to its streaky appearance, or the Indonesian spelling *spekuk*, but most famously it is known as *kue lapis legit* (literally, 'sweet layer cake'). This is my version of Popo's cake, made in a 20cm round cake tin with fewer layers.

Pictured overleaf

Origin Popular all over Indonesia
Serves 24

——

370g unsalted butter, softened, plus extra
   for greasing
150g condensed milk
22 medium egg yolks, at room temperature
150g icing sugar
70g plain flour
25g milk powder
1½ tsp ground cinnamon
¼ tsp ground nutmeg
¼ tsp ground ginger
¼ tsp ground cardamom
¼ tsp sea salt

To make a perfect thousand-layer cake, follow these tips:

- Use only the grill function in the oven and never the fan.

- As the layers get higher you may need to adjust the grilling time or lower the cooking shelf.

- The layer is ready when it has changed from pale to golden.

- Keep an eye on the cake at all times when it is grilling, as it can easily burn.

- Holes will form in the layers if the heat is too high, so adjust the temperature as needed.

- Ideally, each layer should only take between 1½–4 minutes to grill, depending on your oven.

- Ensure even layers by being consistent and measuring each layer; I like to use 5 tablespoons (or 75g) at a time for a 20cm round tin.

Preheat the oven to 200°C/180°C fan/gas 6. Grease a 20cm round cake tin, then line with it baking parchment on the base and sides.

Using an electric whisk, beat the butter with the condensed milk in a mixing bowl until pale and fluffy, about 5 minutes. In a separate bowl and using clean beaters, whisk the egg yolks and icing sugar together until fluffy and doubled in volume. At a low speed, gradually add the egg yolk mixture to the whipped butter about 2 tablespoons at a time, beating between additions, but being careful not to overmix. Sift the flour with the milk powder, spices and salt into the bowl. Using a spatula or large spoon, gently fold through the cake mixture until all the flour is incorporated to create a smooth, streak-free batter.

Switch the oven to the grill function and ensure the fan is turned off. Spread a thin 3mm-thick layer of the batter in the prepared tin so the base is covered. Bang the tin on the work surface to remove any air bubbles. Place on the top shelf of the oven and grill until golden – this may take anywhere between 1½–4 minutes depending on your oven. Remove from the grill, pop any air bubbles that have formed with a cocktail stick and flatten the layer with a fish slice or palette knife. Spread another thin layer of batter on top of the first, about 5 tablespoons, and bang the tin to remove more air bubbles. Grill again for 1½–4 minutes or until the top is golden. Repeat until all the batter is used up, keeping the layers even.

Allow the cake to cool for 30 minutes in the tin. Once cool, remove from the tin and transfer it to a wire rack to cool completely. The cake makes 24 servings as it is incredibly rich, so only a small slice is needed.

BASIC RECIPES

—

WHITE RICE
NASI PUTIH

Serves 4 as a side

—

240g jasmine or basmati rice
½ tsp sea salt

Rinse the rice thoroughly under cold water until it runs clear. Place the rice in a saucepan with 360ml fresh water and the salt. Place the saucepan over a high heat and bring to a slow boil, then reduce the heat to low. Place foil over the saucepan, then place a tight-fitting lid on top and simmer for 15 minutes. Remove from the heat without lifting the lid and leave to stand for 10 minutes. Fluff the grains of rice with a fork and serve immediately.

BROWN RICE
NASI MERAH

Serves 4 as a side

—

240g brown rice
½ tbsp coconut oil or sunflower oil
½ tsp sea salt

Rinse the rice thoroughly under cold water until it runs clear. Heat the oil in a saucepan over a medium-high heat. Add the rice to the pan and stir for a few minutes until it smells fragrant and toasty. Add 480ml fresh water along with the salt and bring to a slow boil. Reduce the heat to low and gently simmer for 30 minutes, uncovered, then remove the pan from the heat. Cover the pan with a tight-fitting lid and leave to stand for 10 minutes. Fluff the grains of rice with a fork and serve immediately.

RED RICE
NASI MERAH

Serves 4 as a side

——

240g red rice
1 tbsp coconut oil or sunflower oil
½ tsp sea salt

Rinse the rice thoroughly under cold water until it runs clear. Heat the oil in a saucepan over a medium-high heat. Add the rice to the pan and stir for a few minutes until it smells fragrant and toasty. Add 480ml fresh water along with the salt and bring to a slow boil. Reduce the heat to low and gently simmer, uncovered, for 30 minutes, ensuring the grains still have a little bite. Remove from the heat, cover the pan with a tight-fitting lid and leave to stand for 10 minutes. Fluff the grains of rice with a fork and serve immediately.

COCONUT RICE
NASI UDUK

Serves 4 as a side

——

240g jasmine or basmati rice
½ tsp sea salt
Pinch of caster sugar
135ml coconut milk mixed with 135ml water

Rinse the rice thoroughly under cold water until it runs clear. Place the rice, salt and sugar in a saucepan with the coconut milk. Place the saucepan over a high heat and bring to a slow boil, then reduce the heat to low. Place foil over the saucepan, then a tight-fitting lid on top. Gently simmer for 15 minutes. Remove from the heat without lifting the lid and leave to stand for 15 minutes. Fluff the grains of rice with a fork and serve immediately.

TURMERIC YELLOW RICE
NASI KUNING

At Indonesian celebrations you will often find the majestic *nasi kuning*, a turmeric-stained golden rice that is placed at the centre of a feast, served in the form of a tall cone called *tumpeng*. Its grand shape mirrors the curves of the mountains and volcanoes found all over Indonesia, and every grain of rice represents the people, with god sitting on top. If you're short of time or ingredients you can omit the aromatics, but adding them gives the rice a luscious flavour that makes it as delicious as it is beautiful.

Serves 4 as a side

240g jasmine or basmati rice
¼ tsp ground turmeric
½ tsp sea salt

Optional aromatics
1 cinnamon stick
6cm piece of ginger (about 30g), peeled and sliced
1 lemongrass stalk, bruised and tied in a knot
1 bay leaf

Place a dry pan over a medium-low heat and toast the cinnamon stick, if using, until it is fragrant. Set aside. Rinse the rice thoroughly under cold water until it runs clear. Stir the ground turmeric and salt into 360ml water until dissolved. Place the rice, cinnamon stick and other aromatics, if using, in a saucepan with the turmeric water. Place the saucepan over a high heat and bring to a slow boil, then reduce the heat to low. Place foil over the saucepan, then a tight-fitting lid on top. Gently simmer for 15 minutes.

Remove from the heat without lifting the lid and leave to stand for 10 minutes. Remove the aromatics, then fluff the grains of rice with a fork and serve immediately.

VEGETABLE STOCK
KALDU SAYUR

Makes 500ml

———

2 tbsp coconut oil or sunflower oil

6 small banana shallots or 12 Thai shallots, peeled and halved lengthways

3 carrots, peeled and chopped into 4cm chunks

3 celery stalks, chopped into 4cm chunks

2 leeks, chopped into 4cm chunks

Spices

1 tbsp black peppercorns

2 tsp coriander seeds

1 tsp cumin seeds

1 star anise

1 cinnamon stick

Aromatics

Handful of coriander stalks

4 garlic cloves, bruised

6cm piece of ginger (about 30g), peeled and thinly sliced

2 lemongrass stalks, bruised and tied in a knot

2 bay leaves

2 kaffir lime leaves (optional)

Place the spices in a dry pan over a medium heat and toast until fragrant. Set aside. Heat the oil in a large, deep saucepan or stock pot over a medium-high heat. Sauté the vegetables in batches until golden, being careful not to burn them. Return all the vegetables to the pan, along with the toasted spices and the aromatics. Add enough cold water to cover and bring to a slow boil. Reduce the heat and simmer for 30 minutes.

Skim off the foamy, brown scum that appears on the surface with a large spoon to prevent the stock from getting cloudy. Top up with more cold water each time you skim. If you find that skimming removes too many of the aromatics, pass the scum through a sieve to return the aromatics to the pan. Once finished, strain the stock through a sieve and return the liquid to a clean saucepan. Reduce the stock over a high heat until the concentration is strong and flavourful.

FISH STOCK
KALDU IKAN

Makes 500ml

———

1.5kg white fish bones (this can include 1 head, rinsed well and cut into large pieces)
6 small banana shallots or 12 Thai shallots, peeled and halved lengthways
3 carrots, peeled and chopped into 4cm chunks
3 celery stalks, chopped into 4cm chunks
2 leeks, chopped into 4cm chunks

Spices
1 tbsp black peppercorns
2 tsp coriander seeds
1 tsp cumin seeds
1 star anise
1 cinnamon stick

Aromatics
Handful of coriander stalks
4 garlic cloves, bruised
6cm piece of ginger (about 30g), peeled and thinly sliced
2 lemongrass stalks, bruised and tied in a knot
2 bay leaves
2 kaffir lime leaves (optional)

Place the spices in a dry pan over a medium heat and toast until fragrant. Place the toasted spices along with all the other ingredients in a large, deep saucepan with enough cold water to cover and bring to a slow boil. Reduce the heat and simmer for 30 minutes.

Skim off the foamy, brown scum that appears on the surface with a large spoon to prevent the stock from getting cloudy. Top up with more cold water each time you skim. If you find that skimming removes too many aromatics, pass the scum through a sieve to return the aromatics to the pan. Once finished, strain the stock through a sieve and return the liquid to a clean saucepan. Reduce the stock over a high heat until the concentration is strong and flavourful.

CHICKEN STOCK
KALDU AYAM

Makes 500ml

———

2 tbsp coconut oil or sunflower oil

6 small banana shallots or 12 Thai shallots, peeled and halved lengthways

3 carrots, peeled and chopped into 4cm chunks

3 celery stalks, chopped into 4cm chunks

2 leeks, chopped into 4cm chunks

2kg chicken bones

Spices

1 tbsp black peppercorns

2 tsp coriander seeds

1 tsp cumin seeds

1 star anise

1 cinnamon stick

Aromatics

Handful of coriander stalks

4 garlic cloves, bruised

6cm piece of ginger (about 30g), peeled and thinly sliced

2 lemongrass stalks, bruised and tied in a knot

2 bay leaves

2 kaffir lime leaves (optional)

Place the spices in a dry pan over a medium heat and toast until fragrant. Set aside. Heat the oil in a large, deep saucepan or stock pot over a medium-high heat. Sauté the vegetables in batches until golden, being careful not to burn them. Return all the vegetables to the pan, along with the chicken bones, toasted spices and aromatics. Add enough cold water to cover and bring to a slow boil. Reduce the heat and simmer for 2–3 hours.

Skim off the foamy, brown scum that appears on the surface with a large spoon to prevent the stock from getting cloudy. Top up with more cold water each time you skim. If you find that skimming removes too many of the aromatics, pass the scum through a sieve to return the aromatics to the pan. Once finished, strain the stock through a sieve and return the liquid to a clean saucepan. Reduce the stock until the concentration is strong and flavourful.

FRIED SHALLOTS
BAWANG MERAH GORENG

I keep a jar of freshly fried shallots or the shop-bought variety in my cupboard as they are the perfect garnish for all savoury Indonesian dishes. Make in large batches, as it keeps for 2 weeks in an airtight container.

—

Makes About 250g

—

500g small banana shallots or Thai shallots, peeled and thinly sliced
Sea salt, to taste
Sunflower oil, for deep-frying

Toss the sliced shallots with a little salt to add flavour. Fill a deep saucepan one-third full with oil. Heat the oil to 140ºC. (If you do not have a kitchen thermometer, check the oil is at temperature by adding a cube of bread; it should turn golden in 40–45 seconds.) Add the shallots and, stirring occasionally, gently cook for 10–12 minutes. When more than half the shallots are golden, turn off the heat and allow the shallots to brown in the residual heat. Remove from the oil with a slotted spoon and spread the fried shallots flat on a tray lined with paper towels. Store in an airtight container at room temperature.

Keep the shallot oil in an airtight container, as it is utterly delicious. I like to stir a little through rice before serving to give a lovely depth of flavour.

FRIED GARLIC
BAWANG PUTIH GORENG

Alongside fried shallots, fried garlic is the perfect garnish. Sprinkle it over soups, noodles and stir-fries, and reserve the garlic oil to make dressings, stir through rice or drizzle over bread. It keeps for several weeks in an airtight container.

—

Makes About 50g

—

2 heads of garlic, cloves peeled and thinly sliced
Sea salt, to taste
Sunflower oil, for deep-frying

Toss the sliced garlic with a little salt to add flavour. Fill a small, deep saucepan one-third full with oil. Heat the oil to 140ºC. (If you do not have a kitchen thermometer, check the oil is at temperature by adding a cube of bread; it should turn golden in 40–45 seconds.) Add the garlic and, stirring occasionally, gently cook for 3 minutes or until the garlic is golden in colour. Remove from the oil with a slotted spoon and spread the fried garlic flat on a tray lined with paper towels.

EGG CREPES
TELUR DADAR

Egg crepes are really popular in Indonesia. A great source of protein, they are stuffed with a delicious filling and rolled like a spring roll (p.46), or served as a garnish or side dish with rice, salads, soups and noodles. You will need a 20cm non-stick pan.

Makes 10 crepes

2 tbsp plain flour
Large pinch of sea salt
4 medium eggs, lightly beaten
Sunflower oil, for frying

Sift the flour and salt into a bowl. Beat the eggs with 4 tablespoons of water and very gradually add them to the flour, about a tablespoon at a time, whisking well after every addition until smooth. Pass the batter through a sieve to remove any lumps (although vigorous whisking should have prevented any from forming).

Place a non-stick frying pan over a medium-low heat. Add ½ teaspoon of oil to the pan, then wipe it out with a paper towel. Add 2 tablespoons of the egg batter to the pan to coat the base very thinly and swirl it around. Smooth it with a teaspoon, if needed, and add extra batter to fill any holes. The crepe will cook in 10–15 seconds. Carefully flip it over using a spatula. Repeat until all the batter has been used. Stack the crepes on top of one another and keep covered in foil.

To serve, roll each egg crepe into a long cylinder and slice into 5mm pieces.

ROASTED FERMENTED SHRIMP PASTE
TERASI BAKAR

Roasting *terasi* brings out its flavour. The technique used here prevents the pungent odour of the shrimps escaping and lingering in your kitchen. Roasted *terasi* lasts a long time, up to the date of expiry on the packaging – just be sure to wrap it in baking parchment and two layers of foil and store it in an airtight container.

250g terasi in a block

Preheat the oven to 180ºC/160ºC fan/gas 4. Slice the terasi block into pieces about 1cm wide. Lay the slices on a large sheet of foil and wrap them so they are completely covered. Place on a tray and bake in the oven for 6 minutes. Remove from the oven and leave to cool in the foil.

BANANA LEAF
DAUN PISANG

Follow this 10-second method to ensure that your banana leaf is pliable before use.

For 1 banana leaf

Using scissors, cut your banana leaf to size and wipe it clean with a damp cloth. Turn the hob on to a medium heat and very quickly pass the leaf over it. You will see the leaf darken and glisten as it hits the heat, so be sure to keep it moving so it doesn't burn. Once the leaf is heated all over on both sides, it is ready to use.

HOMEMADE KECAP MANIS
KECAP MANIS

I adore shop-bought kecap manis, but it can be difficult to find in some general supermarkets. This recipe makes a perfect substitute and, stored in an airtight container, keeps for several weeks in the fridge.

———

Makes About 120ml

———

60ml light soy sauce or gluten-free tamari
90g palm sugar or brown sugar

Combine the soy sauce and sugar in a small saucepan, place over a medium heat and bring to a simmer. Reduce the heat to low and thicken to the consistency of maple syrup. This should take no longer than 5 minutes. Leave to cool.

TAMARIND WATER
AIR ASAM

You can easily buy pre-prepared tamarind paste, but if you want maximum flavour, try making tamarind water using blocks of tamarind pulp. It can be used in the same way as tamarind paste in recipes.

———

Makes About 360ml

———

60g tamarind pulp

Mix the tamarind pulp with 360ml boiling water, stir together and leave for 20 minutes. Strain the pulp through a sieve, pushing out as much liquid as possible. Discard the pulp. Use the tamarind water immediately or freeze any leftovers in ice cube trays for later use.

COCONUT MILK
SANTAN

Shop-bought coconut milk is perfectly fine, but there are two traditional ways to make your own, which are definitely worth the effort and are very common in Indonesia. One uses mature coconut, and the other uses unsweetened desiccated coconut. Fresh *santan* should be used within a day being made, but when frozen it can be kept for up to 3 months.

Makes About 500ml

1 medium mature coconut or
   100g desiccated coconut

Method 1 – Mature coconut

When choosing a coconut, pick one with brown skin and listen for the sound of liquid inside when shaking it. Avoid any that have a greyish hue, and there should be no mould on the three eyes of the coconut. Purchase a medium coconut with the husk removed, or remove and clean it yourself with a knife.

To open the coconut, place your fingers over the three eyes. One of the eyes will feel softer than the other two. Place the tip of a corkscrew or small sharp knife into the softest eye and turn it to make a hole. Pour out the coconut water into a jug. (Drink it, it's delicious!) Place the coconut with its three eyes facing downwards. Find the widest part of the coconut (the equator, as I like to call it) and strongly tap it all the way around with a hammer or a rolling pin. It should crack open after five or six strong taps.

Inside both halves of the coconut you will find thick, firm white flesh. Remove the white coconut flesh using a spoon and a knife. Carefully scrape away the thin brown skin that is attached to the white flesh with a knife. Next, grate the remaining white flesh into a bowl with a cheese grater or pulse it in a food processor until it turns to fine grains. Massage 250ml cold water into the grated coconut for several minutes until the water turns milky white. Strain the liquid through a sieve, preferably lined with muslin, then repeat the process with the same grated coconut flesh and another 250ml cold water.

Method 2 – Desiccated coconut

Place the desiccated coconut in a jug and pour over 500ml boiling water. Using a handheld blender, blitz together and leave to cool. Once cooled, strain through a sieve lined with muslin.

MARTABAK DOUGH
ROTI MARTABAK

Makes 12-16 x 15cm squares

———

500g plain flour
Large pinch of sea salt
1 medium egg, beaten
75ml sunflower oil
Unsalted butter, softened, for coating the dough

Suggested fillings
Egg and spring onion martabak (p.36)
Lamb martabak (p.40)

Sift the flour and salt together in a large bowl. Add the egg and oil to the flour with 125ml cold water, then mix together to make a smooth dough. The dough should have no dry patches and come away easily from the sides of the bowl. If needed, add up to another 50ml water, incorporating only a few drops at a time. Knead the dough for 5 minutes and then form into a ball. If the dough looks too dry, wet your hands with water to add liquid and continue kneading. If it is too wet, sprinkle a little extra flour on the dough as you knead it. Rub the dough all over with softened unsalted butter, then cover with cling film and leave it to rest for 2 hours at room temperature. Once rested, use as instructed in the recipe.

When wrapped in greased cling film and stored in an airtight container, martabak dough can be frozen for up to 3 months. To defrost, remove from the freezer about 2 hours before you need to use it and leave on the counter at room temperature, covered in a bowl.

DUMPLING DOUGH
ROTI CHAI KUE

Makes About 25 dumpling wrappers

———

240g plain flour
Pinch of sea salt

Suggested fillings
Borneo pork and prawn (p.43)
Potato and sweet potato (p.45)

Sift the flour and salt together in a large bowl. Gradually add 120ml boiling water to the flour, stirring everything together with a wooden spoon. Knead the dough for 5 minutes until it is silky, then form into a ball. Cover with cling film and rest for 30 minutes at room temperature.

Roll the ball into a long cylinder and divide into 25 smaller pieces. Cover with a tea towel to prevent them from drying out. Dust your work surface very lightly with flour. Take one of the chunks of dough and roll it into a small ball. Flatten the ball with the palm of your hand, then roll it out into a small circle using a rolling pin. Roll from the centre outwards towards the edge, turning the dough through 90 degrees after every roll, until the circle is 1.5–2mm thick. You should have a round dumpling wrapper after 8 rolls. If you want a perfect circle, cut out the wrapper with a 7cm round cookie cutter.

Keeping the finished wrappers covered with the tea towel, repeat until all the dumpling wrappers are rolled. I store my rolled wrappers between small sheets of baking parchment to prevent them from sticking, but if your kitchen isn't too hot, a generous dusting of flour between each wrapper also works. Don't pile too many on top of each other because the weight of the wrappers will cause them to stick together.

Try to use the rolled dumpling wrappers within 1 hour so they do not dry out.

THE INDONESIAN PANTRY

During my travels around the Indonesian archipelago, as I discovered new dishes and mastered recipes from the generous home cooks who opened their kitchens to me, I found that Indonesians cook entirely by instinct. Rarely are recipes written down and followed; quantities for spice pastes, sambals and even complete dishes are committed to memory, and ingredients are selected and measured by sight, smell, feel and taste. Working by intuition does not work as well in a cookbook, however, especially one whose primary purpose is to introduce readers to a new cuisine, so I have recreated the recipes in my London kitchen and worked out the right quantities of the ingredients available to me in local supermarkets.

In my kitchen, the aroma of shallots, turmeric, lemongrass, kaffir lime, garlic and the unmissable sting of chilli stir the air as they are sautéed, simmered and fried. These aromatics, alongside rice, coconut and sambal, are the essentials of my Indonesian pantry, and the foundations of many of the dishes you will find in this book. If you have them in your kitchen you should be well placed to create most of the dishes. I have also developed some handy substitutes for difficult-to-find ingredients, without compromising on flavour.

A note on spice pastes

At the heart of most Indonesian meals there is a balanced spice paste called a *bumbu*. In traditional kitchens, ingredients are finely chopped and placed in Indonesia's version of the mortar and pestle, known as the *cobek* (mortar) and *ulekan* (pestle). These beautiful disc-shaped bowls are made from hard wood or volcanic stone, and the *ulekan* grinds and crushes the ingredients as they enter the *cobek,* starting with the hardest ingredients and finishing with the softest. Grinding ingredients this way produces a better flavour than a food processor; the pestle pulverises the aromatic compounds of the ingredients, whereas a food processor tears and shreds.

For recipes where a large amount of spice paste is called for, like my Beef rendang (p.166), a food processor will certainly be more efficient. And in this book, for ease and practicality I have suggested using a food processor for all spice pastes, but if you prefer the traditional approach and have time to do so, I do encourage you to go old-school and use a pestle and mortar. It is a satisfying and cathartic process to grind the ingredients yourself, and there will be an advantage in flavour and texture.

The success of your spice paste comes down to three key elements: oil, temperature and time.

Oil A recipe will often call for what seems like a large amount of oil to fry the spice paste in; this will prevent it from drying out and burning, and help the ingredients caramelise. At any stage, if your spice paste is looking too dry, add a splash more oil. When enough oil has been used and the moisture in the ingredients has evaporated, you will see the ingredients begin to split from the oil, which is a sign that the spice paste is ready for the next stage of cooking.

Temperature Always cook your spice paste over a medium heat. Too high and the spice paste will burn and become bitter; too low and the ingredients will simmer and become too sweet.

Time Finally, give your spice paste time. It should take 10–15 minutes (or sometimes less) for a spice paste to cook down and reach its most flavourful and aromatic stage.

On occasion a recipe will not require the spice paste to be cooked off first. With a rendang, the caramelisation of the spices happens at the end of the cooking. In the case of slow-cooked dishes, such as pork ribs, the spice paste cooks and caramelises in the juices of the meat while it cooks in the oven.

A note on toasting and grinding spices

A raw spice and a toasted spice taste very different. The former is lighter and fresh, while a toasted spice adds earthiness and depth to a dish, as well as a crisper texture resulting from the evaporation of any moisture as it is toasted. A delicate fish dish may only need light, raw spices to complement it, while a hearty stew will need toasted spices to add layers of complexity.

Whole spices will always be fresher than ground, so if you have the means, grind your own spices to impart maximum flavour. The best way to grind spices is with a spice or coffee grinder or a mortar and pestle. I keep pre-ground spices in my cupboard for moments when I'm short of time, and it's always handy having a variety of both. When toasting whole spices, add them to a cold, dry pan and move them around continually to stop them burning as the pan begins to heat. Once you can smell the fragrance and the colour begins to darken, the spice is ready. It's best not to toast ground spices as they can burn quickly.

Light and heat are the enemies of spices, so store them safely in a dark cupboard to maximise their shelf life. I prefer not to toast my spices in advance as the flavour of toasted spices begins to deteriorate after a week.

Bay leaf
Daun salam

Indonesian bay leaves, known as *salam* leaves, are used in much the same way as bay leaves in Western cooking, but they taste different. *Salam* adds sweet, earthy flavours to a dish, but as it is difficult to find in the West, I use bay leaves, which have a herbal, pepper and pine fragrance, as a perfect substitute. Fresh or dried bay leaves work in any recipe in this book.

Bean sprouts
Tauge

Grown by sprouting mung beans, bean sprouts have a watery, grassy flavour that adds crunch to stir-fries, noodles, soups and salads. Store bean sprouts in a bowl of water in the fridge, changing the water every day so they don't go slimy. Only eat raw bean sprouts labelled 'ready to eat' – all other varieties should be sautéed, stir-fried or boiled before using.

Candlenut
Kemiri

A waxy, cream-coloured nut with a brittle texture, this relative of the Australian macadamia nut is used in spice pastes for its high oil content, thickening quality and ability to add texture. Slightly toxic when eaten raw, they should be roasted in the oven or toasted in a warm frying pan to draw out their flavour. Candlenuts are available in Asian supermarkets, but you can substitute them for macadamia nuts, raw cashews or almonds. I roast a large batch of candlenuts in the oven at 190ºC/170ºC fan/gas 5 for 12–15 minutes and then store them in an airtight container, ready to be used whenever they are needed.

Chillies
Cabe or cabai

There are hundreds of varieties of chilli. The typical rule of thumb is the smaller the chilli, the hotter it is. The mouth-numbing spiciness comes from capsaicin, a compound found in the white membrane inside the chilli that coats the seeds, but is not present in the seeds themselves. If you have a low chilli tolerance, be sure to remove both the pith and the seeds when deseeding. A great tip when cooking is to reserve the seeds, which gives you the opportunity to add more heat later should the dish need an added kick.

When buying chillies, as a guide, choose varieties that are the length and width of your finger. Most of my recipes call for this type, which gives a moderate heat and becomes milder with pith and seeds removed.

Green chillies are more bitter and raw in taste than red chillies. I use the smaller, hotter bird's eye chillies as a light garnish on sambals or a finished dish. If you are using bird's eye instead of the larger type, I would divide the quantity needed by 4 and deseed if necessary, as the dish will still be hotter.

Dried chillies should be soaked in hot water for 10 minutes to soften them before using.

To protect your hands when preparing chillies, you can coat your hands in oil before touching the chilli, wear disposable gloves or (my favourite option), after touching any chillies, wash your hands in cold, soapy water and rub them on the side of the stainless-steel sink. The molecules in the steel attract the molecules of chilli away from your skin.

Chinese celery leaf
Seledri

Chinese celery leaf is used in the same way as parsley or coriander in other cuisines. Thinner and more pungent than its Western counterpart, it gives a grassy and peppery finish. It's available in Asian supermarkets, but coriander is a good substitute.

Cinnamon
Kayu manis

Highly aromatic, with both sweet and savoury notes, cinnamon is widely used in Indonesian cuisine, often in curries and broths, infusing a mild and warmly spiced flavour. In Indonesia they use Chinese cinnamon bark known as cassia, a more intense cousin of cinnamon available in some Asian supermarkets, but I use cinnamon sticks or bark, which are more widely available. To release the most flavour, toast your cinnamon stick or bark in a frying pan on a medium heat for 2 minutes until it is fragrant and warm to the touch, shaking or stirring the pan continually to prevent burning. Ground cinnamon is used in baked goods like cakes, along with other ground spices such as nutmeg, cardamom and ginger.

Coconut
Kelapa

Indonesia is the world's largest producer of coconuts, and no part of the coconut tree is wasted. Young coconuts produce sweet, fresh coconut water with flesh so tender it falls away with a simple scoop of a spoon. The grated flesh comes from the mature coconut, firm enough to be grated or for the chunks of flesh to be thrown into a food processor. It is this grated flesh that fresh coconut milk, known as *santan* (p.255), comes from. Canned coconut milk with an extract percentage above 50% is an ideal substitute for fresh *santan*. As the thickened coconut cream usually separates from the thinner coconut water, shake the can vigorously before using.

Coriander seeds
Ketumbar

Coriander seeds are one of the most commonly used spices in Indonesian cooking. Used raw, they are floral with a hint of citrus, and when roasted they become strong and earthy. If you have a spice grinder, toast whole seeds in a dry pan over a medium heat until fragrant, then grind them, as this will bring out the best flavour. Otherwise, buy ground coriander, which should be used untoasted, as it can easily burn.

Cumin
Jinten

Cumin imparts a sweet, smoky and earthy flavour in cooking. If you have a spice grinder, toast your seeds in a dry pan over a medium heat until fragrant and then grind them, which will bring out their best flavour for Indonesian cuisine. Otherwise, buy ground cumin which should be used untoasted, as it easily burns.

Curry leaves
Daun kari

Curry leaves are often found in the cuisine of Aceh in Northern Sumatra, thanks to the province's heavy Indian influence due to the traders who passed through the region. Curry leaves are glossy and aromatic, tasting of citrus with a hint of bitterness and a fragrance of curry. It's not related in any form to curry powder, and the best way to bring out its flavour is to cook the leaves in oil. You can eat the leaves when they are added fresh to dishes, although I would avoid eating the dried leaves, which have less aroma and flavour. The fresh variety will keep for up to two weeks in the fridge, but they can also be frozen. When removing from the freezer, bruise the frozen leaves before adding them to the pan to release their flavour.

Dried anchovies
Ikan bilis

Served crispy and deep-fried, dried anchovies are a much-loved staple in Indonesia. They come in a range of sizes, from tiny to finger length. With an irresistible umami-laden taste of the sea that is crunchy, salty and delicious, you will often find dried anchovies eaten as a snack combined with sambal and peanuts, or ground and stirred through a dish for flavour and texture (see the Padang green chilli sambal, p.202). You will find them in the freezer section of most Asian supermarkets. Tinned anchovies are a great substitute.

Dumpling and spring roll wrappers

Dumpling wrappers can be found frozen in Asian supermarkets and at some larger supermarket chains. To use the wrappers, defrost the packet in your fridge for around 2 to 4 hours. Once defrosted, they are best used on the day. Once the packet is open, it is best to cover your unused wrappers with a clean cloth or tea towel to prevent them from drying out when folding your dumplings. Seal your dumplings together by moistening the edges of the wrapper before folding them together. Homemade dumpling wrappers (p.257) should be used within 1 hour once they have been rolled out, but you can freeze any leftover wrappers by dusting each one with plain flour and freezing them in an airtight bag or container. To defrost, thaw the homemade wrappers in the fridge for 1 hour before using.

Frozen spring roll wrappers can also be bought at Asian supermarkets and some supermarket chains, and are available in a variety of sizes. Defrost in the fridge a few hours before use and once the packet is open, store any unused wrappers under a clean cloth or tea towel. They can be sealed using an egg wash (brush beaten egg on the edges of the wrapper with a pastry brush before sealing) or a cut banana (slice a 5cm chunk off an unpeeled banana and rub the exposed end over the wrapper's edges like a glue stick, then seal).

Fish sauce
Kecap ikan

Fish sauce is a condiment that is made from fermented and salted fish. Used in Indonesian cuisine as a seasoning, it imparts a salty, umami flavour to savoury dishes that is often balanced by sugar. Not all fish sauces are created equal, so try to avoid the generic supermarket brands and opt for the specialist fish sauce brands found in Asian supermarkets and some major supermarkets, such as Red Boat, Tiparos or Squid.

Flours

Indonesians use a variety of flours to create the many sweets (*jajanan pasar*) and savoury doughs that form part of their snack culture. The most commonly used flours are rice flour, made from finely milled rice; glutinous rice flour, which is made from milled sweet rice and produces a chewy and sticky texture; and tapioca flour, which is made from the starch of cassava root. Tapioca flour can be substituted for cornflour in my cheese biscuits recipe (p.30), but there is no substitute for glutinous rice flour in my recipe for *klepon*, or glutinous rice balls (p.224). Rice flour can be substituted with plain flour or cake flour at a stretch, although rice flour produces a more tender texture, so the end result will be different.

Fried shallots and fried garlic
Bawang merah goreng dan bawang putih goreng

Crunchy and delicious, thinly sliced, deep-fried shallots and garlic are, for me, the best garnish in the world. Sprinkle them over rice, curries and stir-fries. You can buy them in tubs at Asian supermarkets and some major supermarkets, but for the best flavour, make them yourself (p.251).

Galangal
Lengkuas

A tough and stocky cousin of ginger, galangal has a fresh pine aroma that is sharp and citrusy. It has a woody, textured skin, usually with a pink stem, and you will find younger roots softer to work with. I wash the galangal and use the root and skin whole if fresh; otherwise, the skin can be peeled or sliced to remove the woody exterior. If your galangal is particularly tough, you can soak thin slices in water for 30 minutes before attempting to grind it in a food processor, as tough pieces can be stubborn to chop. Minced galangal in jars can be used as a substitute, or add the equivalent amount of fresh ginger.

Garlic
Bawang putih

Garlic is used both raw and cooked in Indonesian cooking. Thinly sliced lengthways and fried in oil, it becomes a crispy garnish; finely chopped, it flavours stir-fries and spice pastes as the garlic becomes caramelised; sliced thinly and added raw to a sambal, it has a pungent, intense and sharp flavour.

Ginger
Jahe

Ginger provided a zesty heat in Indonesian cuisine long before chillies arrived with Portuguese traders in the sixteenth century. The yellow root is covered in a skin that can be peeled with a teaspoon. Fresh ginger is best, as pre-minced ginger can give an artificial taste, and ground ginger is not suitable for Indonesian cooking.

Kaffir lime leaves
Daun jeruk purut

Alongside lemongrass, kaffir lime is one of my favourite scents. Fresh or frozen are best, or alternatively you can use dried kaffir lime leaves, although they will not have the same strength of flavour and tend to crumble a little during the cooking process.

They can be found in Asian stores and some major supermarkets and, while there is no true substitute for the fresh and zingy kaffir lime leaf, you can add extra flavour with ½ bay leaf or 1 curry leaf in its place. The juice and zest of the kaffir lime fruit is divine, but can be substituted with ordinary limes.

Kecap manis

A sweetened soy sauce with the aroma of spices such as cloves, coriander and black pepper. A thick syrup with the texture of molasses, kecap manis is most commonly used as a marinade, drizzled over a finished dish or as a seasoning. It's available in large supermarkets, but if you can't find it in your local shops, or you need a gluten-free variety, you can make your own simplified homemade version (p.254).

Lemon basil
Daun kemangi

Lemon basil tastes and smells just like the name suggests. Its perfume has a remarkable ability to transform a dish, giving it freshness and the unmistakable taste of basil and citrus. Lemon basil can be quite difficult to source in general supermarkets, in which case the best substitutes are Thai basil, holy basil or Italian basil.

Lemongrass
Serai

One of my favourite flavours, lemongrass is a tall tropical grass that contains citral, the same essential oil found in lemon peel, which gives it an intensely fragrant lemony flavour. In Indonesia it is used as a skewer for minced satays, and is also bruised and added to slow-cooked dishes to impart its flavour gradually. If finely chopped and used in spice pastes or stir-fries, always remove the outer two leaves before cutting, as they can be woody. If bruising lemongrass, I like to bash it thoroughly with the blunt side of the knife, then tie it into a knot to prevent it from disintegrating during cooking.

Light soy sauce
Kecap asin

Light soy sauce is commonly added as a seasoning to Chinese-influenced dishes in Indonesia. When buying soy sauce, it is important to distinguish light from dark as the two have very different uses: dark soy sauce is aged for longer with molasses and is used as a marinade or dipping sauce, whereas light soy sauce is saltier, thinner and used as a light seasoning. Gluten-free light soy is available in the form of tamari.

Limes
Jeruk nipis

The juice and rinds of limes are indispensable in Indonesian cuisine, used to season sauces, spice pastes, sambals and a variety of other dishes. Wedges of lime are served as a garnish to season dishes such as soups, along with sambal and kecap manis.

Martabak dough

For an authentic *martabak* eaten at home, make your own dough (p.256). The martabak ingredients are combined into a dough and then rested before being rolled out on an oiled surface. You can freeze your martabak dough for up to 3 months covered in greased cling film in an airtight container. Defrost at room temperature for 2 hours before using. Spring roll wrappers or filo pastry work as good substitutes for homemade martabak dough, and although the end result will be different, it will still be delicious.

Morning glory
Kangkung

Also known as water spinach, morning glory is considered a weed in some parts of the world because of its ability to grow anywhere that has plenty of water. It needs to be washed thoroughly and should never be eaten raw, as it can contain a parasite on its leaves that is eliminated through cooking. Best stir-fried, boiled or steamed with plenty of spices and seasoning to add flavour, it's available in Asian supermarkets but can be substituted with pak choi, spinach or kale.

Nutmeg
Pala

One of the spices indigenous to Indonesia, nutmeg is best bought whole and grated fresh when you need it, but a pinch of the ground spice will work too.

Noodles

All the noodles that feature in this cookbook can be purchased in most supermarkets and Asian supermarkets. Always follow the packet instructions to bring your noodles to life. They can easily be substituted with whichever noodles you have to hand in your pantry, such as rice or egg noodles or soba, although it's generally best to use a noodle as close as possible to the shape specified in the recipe.

Rice vermicelli

Very thin rice noodles served in soup dishes such as *soto* (p.68) all over Indonesia.

Flat rice noodles

These rice noodles are often served in stir-fries such as *kwetiau* (p.184) from Medan, or in soups. The noodles are sold by width, often 5mm, but you can use whatever width you can find in your local supermarket.

Egg noodles

You'll find egg noodles in soup dishes and stir-fries all over the archipelago – most typically in the nationally loved dish of *mie goreng* (p.132), a noodle stir-fry served with a variety of vegetables, seafoods or meats and commonly seasoned with kecap manis. The noodles come in all shapes and sizes, from thick and round to flat, and can be purchased dried, fresh in the fridge or frozen.

Instant noodles

Instant noodles are known by the noodle brand name Indomie in Indonesia, and you'll find street-food and fast-food vendors advertising the name on shop fronts all over the country. Made from wheat flour, these dried curly noodles are typically rehydrated and cooked in boiling water in just a few minutes before being dressed in a variety of flavours and garnishes that transforms them into an exciting bowl of comfort food (p.186).

Oil
Minyak

Due to the overwhelming deforestation of Indonesia and subsequent loss of endangered wildlife and their habitats to make space for palm oil plantations, it's important to source your oil ethically. Palm oil is often labelled as vegetable oil, so it's important to check labels before purchasing. If the label states the amount of saturated fat it is likely to be palm oil, as other vegetable oils are not saturated. Sunflower, canola, grapeseed and rapeseed oils are all great alternative neutral oils. Never use olive oil for Indonesian cooking, as the flavours will clash.

Coconut oil is Indonesia's preferred choice of oil for cooking and is great for deep-frying at temperatures below 170°C, but if you need to fry at a higher temperature than this, use a frying oil such as sunflower. In cooler temperatures, coconut oil solidifies, so do not use it when a drizzle of oil is required to finish a dish, or for any dishes that are served cold or room temperature. Buy fair-trade coconut oil whenever possible to support the growers.

Pak choi

Also known by the name bok choy, pak choi is a type of Chinese cabbage that is widely used in Indonesian cuisine. The green brassica lends itself to a quicker style of cooking – typically sautéed in a couple of minutes or warmed in soups before serving. The whole vegetable can be eaten, apart from the stem. Pak choi works as a wonderful side dish with most savoury dishes in this book.

Palm sugar
Gula merah

There are two main types of palm sugar in Indonesia: palm sugar from the *arenga* palm tree and coconut palm sugar from the coconut tree. The variety used in any given Indonesian home largely depends on which species of tree grows in the local area. Both palm sugars have

nothing to do with palm oil, which has had a devastating effect on the natural environment and animal welfare due to heavy deforestation. Rather, the extraction of palm sugar promotes sustainability, as the trees will yield the palm sugar nectar for more than 100 years, and the life of the tree is pivotal to the production of sugar, so they are preserved and maintained.

Palm sugar producers climb a terrifying thirty metres without any safety equipment, where the surface of the flower buds of the tree is sliced with a sharp blade to release its nectar. It is lusciously caramel in flavour, with tones of molasses, and is used in both savoury and sweet cooking, whether shaved, grated or cut into chunks. You can purchase palm sugar in disc or granulated form, but dark brown sugar works as a great substitute.

Pandan leaf
Daun pandan

Known as the vanilla of the East, the soft, soothing and sweet-smelling aroma of the pandan leaf is found in dishes all over Indonesia, both sweet and savoury. Used to perfume steamed or simmered dishes as well as sweet treats, its trademark presence comes through the extraction of pandan juice by finely shredding the leaves. This imparts a natural green colouring as well as flavour to white ingredients such as flours and rice.

Also called screw pine, the leaves can be purchased fresh, dried or frozen in Asian supermarkets. Pandan is also available in essence, extract or paste form, although I prefer not to use these in baking, as the flavour can be quite artificial and they can impart a lurid green colour to your baked goods. The fresh leaves provide the most flavour and colour, and you can freeze leftover leaves, which can be used for up to a month. If using frozen pandan, you may need to double or triple the quantity of leaves used, as freezing reduces its aroma and flavour. If you cannot find pandan, I have provided natural substitutes in those recipes, such as vanilla or raspberry, which, although different, will produce equally delicious results.

Peanuts
Kacang

Traditionally, Indonesians cook with raw, skin-on peanuts, which they deep-fry whole until they are golden and crispy. If you aren't a fan of frying, you can roast them in the oven or toast them in a hot pan, or use shop-bought unsalted roasted peanuts.

Rice vinegar

Rice vinegar is commonly used in Indonesian cooking for pickling, seasoning and in marinades. It has a milder, sweeter flavour than distilled white vinegar, but can be very successfully substituted with white wine vinegar. You can find rice vinegar in most major supermarkets and Asian supermarkets.

Shallots
Bawang merah

Despite their pungency when raw, shallots become mild and sweet when softened and caramelised. Indonesians use a locally grown variety, but Thai, French or banana shallots are suitable replacements. For the recipes in this book I have given the option of Thai or banana shallots; the latter are easier to find, and to peel, than their smaller Asian counterparts.

Spring onions
Daun bawang

A grassy garnish with a palatable onion flavour, spring onions are perfect when thinly sliced on the diagonal. Indonesians will often add sliced spring onions to stir-fries, use them to flavour soups or serve them raw in salads.

Star anise
Bunga lawang

Star anise is a spice that imparts an aniseed flavour into the broths, stocks and stews it is cooked with. To prepare, toast the star anise in a frying pan over a medium heat for a couple of minutes until fragrant, ensuring you shake or stir the pan to prevent it from burning.

Stock
Kaldu

Making your own stock is worth the effort, and I've provided recipes for vegetable, fish and chicken varieties (pp.248–50). Stored in the freezer, stock will keep for 6 months. If using shop-bought stock, always opt for a good-quality liquid stock if you can, or a concentrated stock pot. Avoid powdered stock cubes as they tend to be too salty.

Tamarind
Asam

The tamarind tree is a thing of beauty. Long, pea-shaped brown pods hang from its thin branches, which swing delicately beside the dainty leaves that form small feather-like fans around the tree. The word for tamarind is *asam* in Indonesian, meaning 'sour', but it is very different from lemon or lime as its sourness is balanced by the pulp's sweetness.

Tamarind comes in a few forms: squeezed straight from the pod as a pulp to make tamarind water (p.254) or ready-to-use as tamarind paste. The strength of a paste really depends on the quality so, if you aren't sure, add a little at a time as a seasoning until it is just right. If you can't find tamarind in your supermarket, substitute it with a mixture of equal parts lime juice and brown sugar.

Tempeh
Tempe

When the Chinese brought soybeans to Indonesia hundreds of years ago, the Indonesians made tempeh, one of the world's greatest superfoods. A rich source of protein, the soybeans are fermented in banana leaves, producing a textured block that is nutty and earthy. It is best cooked cut into chunks and deep-fried or shallow-fried in oil to crisp up its exterior, marinated in kecap manis and grilled, or pan-fried in long strips. If you cannot find tempeh in your local supermarket you can substitute it with smoked, fried, marinated or firm tofu.

Fermented shrimp paste
Terasi

Also known as *belacan*, *terasi* is made from fermented prawns and comes in a dark-brown-coloured block. With its strong fishy odour, it's used in very small quantities, and is usually roasted, fried or grilled to bring out its umami flavour. *Terasi* should be crumbled and then mixed thoroughly with the other ingredients as they cook. The best way to store *terasi* is wrapped in baking parchment and covered in two layers of foil, then kept inside an airtight container. You can find my method for roasting *terasi* on p.253.

Terasi is widely available in Indonesia but can only be found in specialist Asian supermarkets outside of it. Thankfully, it can be substituted with other umami-laden ingredients, such as anchovies, shrimp paste, fish sauce, tomato paste and sun-dried tomatoes. Any of these work well as a substitute provided you add a little at a time as a seasoning, tasting as you go.

Tofu
Tahu

Tofu provides a cheap source of protein for Indonesians, and has been embedded in the food culture since the Chinese introduced it hundreds of years ago. Indonesians often use bean curd, but it is perfectly fine to use any type of tofu you can get your hands on. My personal favourite is smoked tofu, which imparts an irresistible smokiness to dishes. Firm tofu should be drained of liquid and pressed between paper towels to absorb any excess liquid before being marinated in soy or kecap manis. Fried tofu is like a sponge

that soaks up all the flavours of the sauce it is bathed in, creating an explosion of taste with every bite, and can be found in most Asian supermarkets.

Turmeric
Kunyit

This cousin of root ginger has a brown skin on the outside that is peeled away to reveal a hand-staining bright orange interior, which is tangy and bitter with a hint of mustard. It gives yellow rice its sunlit colour and many spice pastes their golden hue. It's also an antioxidant that acts as an anti-inflammatory. If you cannot find fresh turmeric, you can substitute it very successfully with ground turmeric at a ratio of 1 teaspoon for every 3cm or 15g of fresh turmeric. Use turmeric sparingly, however, as its bitterness and ability to turn dishes yellow can easily overpower a dish in both flavour and appearance.

Turmeric stains skin, tea towels, porous surfaces and chopping boards – in fact, just about anything it encounters – so wear gloves when using fresh turmeric, and wash any stains immediately in cold water with liquid soap. Blot stubborn stains with lemon juice, vinegar and coarse sea salt, scrubbing in a circular motion.

PLANNING A MEAL

How to eat like an Indonesian

The key to creating a delicious Indonesian meal is balance – of textures, produce and flavours. A traditional Indonesian meal will feature a selection of vegetable, meat and fish dishes that are prepared in different ways, such as steaming, frying or sautéing. Dishes are served with varying spice levels, and richly flavoured dishes are often complemented by a pickle, whereas more subtle meals rise to new heights with an accompanying fiery sambal. Rice, *kerupuk* crackers and sambal are staples at every meal, so I suggest always serving these at any food gathering.

A bountiful spread of generous dishes are laid down all at once, banquet style, with guests helping themselves and refilling their plates several times, a custom that shows you are enjoying the meal. In many households, the food is laid out in the morning, and is picked at throughout the day, at both lunch and dinner, and it is perfectly acceptable to eat food at room temperature. Any leftovers that will keep are reheated for tomorrow's spread. For special occasions, I suggest enjoying Indonesian food the traditional way, in which a variety of dishes are served and guests can help themselves. For a simpler meal, Indonesian mains are perfect with a side dish of rice or noodles, greens and a sambal. Other dishes such as soups, stir-fries or fried rice will be satisfying to eat on their own, or with a little side of *kerupuk*.

The most traditional way of eating food is with your right hand, and never with your left, which is considered unhygienic. However, as Indonesia has modernised, all meals are now served with a fork and a spoon, which is the best way to scoop up your rice and any leftover sauce swimming on your plate.

How to plan a meal

For serving quantities, aim to serve one dish per person, along with rice, sambal and *kerupuk* on the side, with one extra dish if you anticipate hungry guests. For example, if you had 6 guests you could serve a savoury snack, two vegetables dishes, a noodle dish or stir-fry, a slow-cooked main and a dessert, as well as rice, *kerupuk* and sambal. If you are time-poor you can reduce the number of shared dishes and increase the quantities of each item you cook.

Tips for designing a menu

- Consider texture, which Indonesians find stimulates the appetite. Curate menus that feature the crunch of peanuts, a crispy, fried snack, a thickened curry and the flaky flesh of fish, for example.
- Ensure there are ample amounts of rice and sambal for guests. These are easy to prepare and make an Indonesian meal shine.
- Balance your flavours with a mix of spicy and mild dishes, a pickle to cut through the richness of a meal, or something sour and sweet.
- Choose a menu with some dishes that can be prepared in advance and reheated, and only one that needs to be prepared last minute (such as a fish dish or a stir-fry) so that you aren't rushed before guests arrive.
- We eat with our eyes, so serve a variety of colours, from green vegetables to yellow rice or a brightly coloured sambal.
- Allow your guests to self-season with garnishes like lime wedges, kecap manis and sambal, where appropriate.

MENUS

Vegan spreads

Potato and sweet potato dumplings
    (variation) p.45
Vegetable nasi goreng (omit fried egg) p.80
Soy mushrooms and pak choi p.98
Tofu satay (variation) p.140
Vegan butternut ribs (variation) p.178
Coconut sticky rice balls p.224

or

Vegan martabak (variation) p.40
Balinese coconut lawar salad p.94
Fragrant stir-fried morning glory
    (vegan variation) p.100
Sweet soy tempeh p.106
Spicy baked aubergine p.110
Vegan coconut panna cotta (variation) p.230

——

Pescetarian menus

Egg and spring onion martabak p.36
Gado-gado salad with peanut sauce p.92
Fish and prawn lemongrass satay p.120
Pan-fried dabu-dabu sea bass p.130
Pandan crepes p.216

or

Vegetarian croquettes (variation) p.51
Medanese prawn bisque with noodles p.62
Crispy fish with sambal bawang p.128
Timorese tomato and coriander salad p.96
Peanut and banana ice cream p.228

Summer barbecues

Grilled sweet chilli corn p.34
Timorese tomato and coriander salad p.96
Spice Islands ceviche p.118
Kecap manis calamari p.124
Chicken satay with peanut sauce p.140
Coconut and lime ice cream p.227

or

Pickled sweet and sour coleslaw p.90
Gado-gado salad with peanut sauce p.92
Chilli prawn satay with rica-rica p.122
Oven-baked fish with sambal (barbecue
    variation) p.126
Egg crepe rolls p.156
Pandan and coconut cake p.238

——

Winter feasts

Potato fritters p.31
Chicken nasi goreng p.77
Beef rendang p.166
Stir-fried vegetable cap cay p.102
Sticky ginger toffee pudding p.236

or

Vegetable spring rolls (variation) p.47
Cucumber, chilli and shallot pickle p.88
Spiced meatball soup p.72
Fragrant stir-fried morning glory p.100
Acehnese lamb curry p.188
Banana fritters p.222

Celebration menus

Spiced corn fritters p.32
Fried shallot and coconut rice p.76
Timorese tomato and coriander salad p.96
Crispy soy and ginger roast potatoes p.108
Balinese roasted pork belly p.180
Chilli chocolate and nut caramel tart p.232

or

Chicken and garlic spring rolls p.46
Turmeric pickle p.89
Fried chilli corn p.97
Soy mushrooms and pak choi p.98
Balinese sticky glazed pork ribs p.176
Thousand-layer cake p.240

or

Lamb and potato croquettes p.50
Stir-fried vegetable cap cay p.102
Prawn and chicken fried noodles p.132
Sticky beef short rib with chilli p.172
Palm sugar slice p.235

—

Quick and easy meals

Timorese fish soup p.66
Chicken nasi goreng p.77
Timorese tomato and coriander salad p.96
Fried chilli corn p.97
Sweet soy tempeh p.106
Spicy baked aubergine p.110
Fish and prawn lemongrass satay p.120
Chilli prawn satay with rica-rica p.122
Pan-fried dabu-dabu sea bass p.130
Prawn and chicken fried noodles p.132
Stir-fried Sumba chicken p.146
Acehnese chicken with curry leaves p.152
Green chilli and lemongrass pork p.179
Pork and prawn rice noodles p.184
Crispy pork belly instant noodles p.186

Healthy and light meals

Aubergine and mushroom soup p.60
Medanese prawn bisque with noodles p.62
Woku monkfish stew p.65
Timorese fish soup p.66
Aromatic chicken noodle soto p.68
Pickled sweet and sour coleslaw p.90
Gado-gado salad with peanut sauce p.92
Balinese coconut lawar salad p.94
Timorese tomato and coriander salad p.96
Fried chilli corn p.97
Stir-fried vegetable cap cay p.102
Spicy baked aubergine p.110
Fish and prawn lemongrass satay p.120
Chilli prawn satay with rica-rica p.122
Oven-baked fish with sambal p.126
Pan-fried dabu-dabu sea bass p.130
Stir-fried Sumba chicken p.146
Acehnese chicken with curry leaves p.152
Egg crepe rolls p.156
Green chilli and lemongrass pork p.179

—

Meals that can be prepared in advance

Aubergine and mushroom soup p.60
Aromatic chicken noodle soto p.68
Chicken rice congee p.71
Spiced meatball soup p.72
Betawi beef and coconut soup p.74
Gado-gado salad with peanut sauce p.92
Stir-fried vegetable cap cay p.102
Green chilli braised duck p.154
Beef rendang p.166
Sticky beef short rib with chilli p.172
Sweet soy pork belly p.175
Balinese sticky glazed pork ribs p.176
Acehnese lamb curry p.188

DIETARY LISTS

List of vegetarian recipes

Some of these recipes contain fish sauce, but you can replace this with soy sauce to make them vegetarian.

Peanut and kaffir lime kerupuk p.28
Cheese biscuits p.30
Potato fritters p.31
Spiced corn fritters p.32
Grilled sweet chilli corn p.34
Egg and spring onion martabak p.36
Vegan martabak (variation) p.40
Potato and sweet potato dumplings
    (variation) p.45
Vegetable spring rolls (variation) p.47
Vegetarian croquettes (variation) p.51
Aubergine and mushroom soup p.60
Fried shallot and coconut rice p.76
Vegetable nasi goreng p.80
Cucumber, chilli and shallot pickle p.88
Turmeric pickle p.89
Pickled sweet and sour coleslaw p.90
Balinese coconut lawar salad p.94
Timorese tomato and coriander salad p.96
Soy mushrooms and pak choi p.98
Fragrant stir-fried morning glory
    (use soy sauce and sesame oil) p.100
Stir-fried vegetable cap cay (use soy sauce
    and sesame oil) p.102
Vegetable and tempeh fried noodles p.103
Sweet soy tempeh p.106
Crispy soy and ginger roast potatoes p.108
Spicy baked aubergine p.110
Tofu satay (variation) p.140
Egg crepe rolls p.156
Fried spiced soft-boiled eggs p.158
Vegan butternut ribs (variation) p.178
Tomato sambal p.194

Fresh tomato and basil dabu-dabu p.196
Soy, garlic and chilli dipping sauce p.198
Ground chilli sambal ulek p.199
Caramelised shallot sambal bawang p.200
Peanut sauce p.204
Fresh Balinese sambal matah p.206
Sulawesi rica-rica chilli sauce p.209
Pandan crepes p.216
Indonesian cinnamon doughnuts p.218
Banana fritters p.222
Coconut sticky rice balls p.224
Coconut and lime ice cream p.227
Peanut and banana ice cream p.228
Coconut panna cotta with mango
    (variation) p.230
Chilli chocolate and nut caramel tart p.232
Palm sugar slice p.235
Sticky ginger toffee pudding p.236
Pandan and coconut cake p.238
Thousand-layer cake p.240

List of vegan recipes

Some of these recipes contain fish sauce, but you can replace this with soy sauce to make them vegan.

Peanut and kaffir lime kerupuk p.28
Vegan martabak (variation) p.40
Potato and sweet potato dumplings
    (variation) p.45
Vegetable spring rolls (variation) p.47
Aubergine and mushroom soup p.60
Fried shallot and coconut rice p.76
Cucumber, chilli and shallot pickle p.88
Turmeric pickle p.89
Pickled sweet and sour coleslaw p.90
Balinese coconut lawar salad p.94

———

List of dairy-free recipes

List of gluten-free recipes

*Some of these recipes contain soy sauce, but
you can replace this with tamari to make them
gluten free. Some contain kecap manis, but
see p.254 for a gluten-free alternative. Some
gluten-free ingredients such as cornflour, rice
flour or tamarind can contain small amounts
of gluten, so always check the packaging.*

INDEX

ACKNOWLEDGEMENTS

This book was written in memory of my grandmother
Margaret Thali, who we called Popo, and my grandfather
Ang Tju Liong. Your technicolour home and vibrant
recipes have a place in my heart forever.

The idea for this cookbook was born out of a desire to know my father's culture and become immersed in our heritage. To my parents Jono and Coralie Agung – I owe you the world. Your sacrifices laid the universe at my feet (a childhood peppered with batik, sequinned tutus and limitless opportunities). You taught me the art of dreaming big. To my aunties Kristina, Lily and Linda Agung – I am so grateful to you all for helping me to bring Popo's recipes to life again. Thank you for travelling with me in Indonesia; this cookbook's story is as much yours as it is mine. A special shout out goes to Aunty Lie Tje Ie for sharing our family stories and recipes with me in her beautiful blue-tiled kitchen. To my sister Katrina and the King family – Anthony, Toby, Penny and Summer – thank you for making my world a brighter place. To the Wood family – Caroline and Jonathan – for all the taste tests and helping me wash up as I used every pot and pan in your kitchen when recipe testing, and also for raising the most beautiful human I have ever known, my husband – big Nick. Thank you, Nick, for the beautiful, intricate hand-drawn map of Indonesia you made for me – what a treasure it is to look upon. From the very beginning you have had unwavering belief in me. Whenever I doubted myself, you lifted me and guided my way. Your patience, love and encouragement have meant the world. To our son Jonah, who spent nine months eating all of these recipes in my womb, I can't wait to show you Popo's home in Timor one day. I love you both.

Many kitchens became a second home to me in the making of this cookbook, but there was none more important than the kitchen of Sri Owen, my culinary mentor. My greatest thanks must go to her for her wisdom and generous teachings, which gave me the confidence to share Indonesian food with the world.

To William Wongso – your passion and never-ending efforts to elevate Indonesian food to the global stage is a constant inspiration. You have been one of my strongest influences as you generously donated your time and knowledge to guide my research, and I thank you from the bottom of my heart.

I would like to offer a heartfelt thanks to my agent Niki Chang for the constant support and encouragement. Also, to Helen Goh – you deserve a special acknowledgement for your thoughtful introductions and belief in me. To Fuchsia Dunlop and Betty Yao at the Yan-kit So Award – your encouragement was a great motivation, so thank you. Special thanks also go to Jeremy Pang for inspiring me and believing in me.

I am deeply grateful to Bloomsbury Publishing for bringing my story to life. To Xa Shaw Stewart and Richard Atkinson, thank you for loving my proposal and embracing my ideas. To my editors Natalie Bellos and Lena Hall, I have loved every minute we worked together. The words in this book shine bright thanks to your guidance. Thank you also to Lisa Pendreigh and Laura Gladwin for your incredible work and meticulous contributions, to Laura Brodie for your hard work in production and to Kitty Stogdon for your organisation behind the scenes. To Ellen Williams, Don Shanahan and Maud Davies, I am grateful for your efforts in promoting this book to the world. I feel extremely lucky to work with you all.

To my creative collaborators: Louise Hagger, Alexander Breeze, Emily Kydd, Laura Heckford, Alice Ostan, and Tim Balaam and Kate Sclater of Hyperkit. Thank you for so beautifully taking the brief of recreating my grandmother's home in the studio and reimagining the lesser-known side of Indonesia that I love. To my photography team – we will always have *batik realness*.

In Indonesia – to Lisa and Mike Bell – your boundless generosity provided a home away from home for me. Special thanks must go to Melanie Jappy for her introduction. Great thanks also go to Ibu Ley Hoen Yoe – you are a culinary master. An immense amount of thanks must also go to: Ratna Kurniawati, Danielle Anindata, Eko Hadiwijaya, Nanik S Taufik, Benny Santoso, Ibu Djelantik,

Ubud Food Festival, Pak Darta and Ibu Tirta, I Putu Dodik Sumarjana, Kieran Morland, Chio, Yen and Min from Depot Selera in Kupang, Timor, Ibu Emmy Pratini, Mami Benny, Professor Murdijati Gardjito, Heni Pridia, Mulyasari Hadiati, Shinta Teviningrum, Firta Hapsari, Kevindra Soemantri, Santhi Serad, Ade Putri, Ibu Amanda Niode, Chindy Lie, Pak Budi Mulharjum and his family (Iwit, Grandma Erneti and Elfira), Uda Dian Anugrah, Indra Halim, Chef Budiman Brata Yada, Ibu Fatimah Kalla, Ibu Soraya, Ibu Maudia Marzuki, Ibu Bernadeth Ratulangi, Dr Leonard Ratulangi, Annie at the Gardenia Country Inn, Ibu Agung, Lily Koo, Kartika Sulistiowati, Trias Susanti and to Siana Rahardjo for the beautiful batik.

To Fiona Hannah, my Kiwi and co-founder of our catering business Kiwi & Roo – my deepest thanks for your encouragement and friendship. Tasting and testing and moral support thanks must also go to Laura Wilson and Matt Reuther, Bridhe McGroder, Ben Stuart, Chris Van Der Walt, Felicity Price Thomas, Tom and Katy Rickey, Will Verdino, Alison and Sarah at Leiths List, Mary Lees, Gill Lambert and Geoff Shearcroft, Keiichi and Asami Matsuda, Dave Rieser and Jen Desmond, Katsura Leslie and Peter Baeck, Abbie Whitehead and Dunstan James, and Nina Gerada and Jon Hagos.

Finally, to the countless street-food vendors, *warung* owners and market sellers who I spoke to and photographed but whose names I never knew, thank you for sharing your skills and knowledge with me and for your kindness. Meeting you painted Indonesian food culture in so many beautiful shades.

LARA LEE is an Indonesian and Australian chef and food writer. She trained at Leiths School of Food and Wine and now runs an event catering business called Kiwi & Roo, serving delicious food to high-profile guests including the royal family and the Australian prime minister; and at venues such as the Natural History Museum and the Royal Academy of Arts. She also holds supper clubs all over London that celebrate her heritage with both Australian and Indonesian cuisine. *Coconut & Sambal* is her first cookbook.

BLOOMSBURY PUBLISHING
Bloomsbury Publishing Plc
50 Bedford Square, London WC1B 3DP, UK

BLOOMSBURY, BLOOMSBURY PUBLISHING
and the Diana logo are trademarks of Bloomsbury
Publishing Plc

First published in Great Britain 2020

Text © Lara Lee, 2020
Recipe photographs © Louise Hagger, 2020
Travel photographs © Lara Lee, 2020
Map on pages 4–5 © Nick Wood at How About
Studio, 2020

Lara Lee, Louise Hagger and Nick Wood have
asserted their right under the Copyright, Designs
and Patents Act, 1988, to be identified as author,
photographer and illustrator respectively of
this work.

For legal purposes the Acknowledgements on
pages 284–5 constitute an extension of this
copyright page.

A catalogue record for this book is available from
the British Library.

ISBN: HB: 978-1-5266-0351-7
eBook: 978-1-5266-0352-4

10 9 8 7 6 5 4 3 2

Project editors: Lisa Pendreigh and Laura Gladwin
Designer: Hyperkit
Food photographer: Louise Hagger
Travel photographer: Lara Lee
Food stylist: Emily Kydd
Prop stylist: Alexander Breeze
Map illustrator: Nick Wood at How About Studio
Indexer: Vanessa Bird

Printed and bound in China by RR Donnelley.

Bloomsbury Publishing Plc makes every effort to
ensure that the papers used in the manufacture
of our books are natural, recyclable products
made from wood grown in well-managed forests.
Our manufacturing processes conform to the
environmental regulations of the country of origin.

To find out more about our authors and books
visit www.bloomsbury.com and sign up for our
newsletters.